Oppression and
the Human Condition

Oppression and the Human Condition

An Introduction to Sartrean Existentialism

Thomas Martin

ROWMAN & LITTLEFIELD PUBLISHERS, INC.
Lanham • Boulder • New York • Oxford

ROWMAN & LITTLEFIELD PUBLISHERS, INC.

Published in the United States of America
by Rowman & Littlefield Publishers, Inc.
A Member of the Rowman & Littlefield Publishing Group
4720 Boston Way, Lanham, Maryland 20706
www.rowmanlittlefield.com

PO Box 317
Oxford
OX2 9RU, UK

British Library Cataloguing in Publication Information Available

Library of Congress Cataloging-in-Publication Data

Martin, Thomas, 1964–
    Oppression and the human condition : an introduction to Sartrean existentialism /
Thomas Martin.
        p. cm.
    Includes bibliographical references and index.
    ISBN 0-7425-1323-8 (alk. paper)—ISBN 0-7425-1324-6 (pbk. : alk. paper)
    1. Sartre, Jean Paul, 1905– 2. Oppression (Psychology) 3. Existentialism. I. Title.
    B2430.S34 M365 2002
    194—dc21   2002007400

Printed in the United States of America

In memory of Bill and Shirley Dibden

Contents

Acknowledgments

Many people and institutions have contributed, in a variety of ways, to the completion of this project. When I began work on Sartre and, as it turned out, on this book, I was a doctoral student, mainly in the School of Philosophy at the University of New South Wales, Australia (though also at Flinders University, Australia, and Uppsala University, Sweden). I owe a great debt of gratitude to my dissertation supervisors at UNSW, Rosalyn Diprose and Genevieve Lloyd. Their support and advice were invaluable, and their philosophical expertise and integrity inspiring. Two of my colleagues at that time, Bill Tarrant and Matthew Paull, also deserve thanks for the many hours of brainstorming we shared. I appreciate the support that was given to me by UNSW and by the Australian government, which funded my studies.

I completed this project at Rhodes University, South Africa, initially as a research fellow, and then as a lecturer. I am grateful to Rhodes University for financially supporting my research throughout this time. I also thank my colleagues in the Department of Philosophy at Rhodes (Ward Jones, Marius Vermaak, Francis Williamson, and Merle Murray) for providing a supportive work environment conducive to philosophical discussion and research. Thanks also go to Samantha Naidu, who proofread the manuscript and provided me with much-needed encouragement in the final stages of the project; to Eve De-Varo and Mary Svikhart from Rowman & Littlefield for good advice and displays of patience; to my family (Anne, Bruce, Rosemary, Peter, and Cathy Martin, and Selma Burne) for love and support; and to Scott MacArthur, Ulrika Hammar, Helen Dampier, and many other friends for . . . well . . . being friends.

Permission to quote was kindly granted by the following publishers.

Taylor & Francis and Georges Borchardt (on behalf of Editions Gallimard) for Jean-Paul Sartre, *Being and Nothingness: An Essay on Phenomenological Ontology.* Translated by Hazel E. Barnes. London: Routledge, 1958. (Originally published as *L'Etre et le Néant.* Paris: Gallimard, 1943.)

Schocken Books, a division of Random House, Inc., for Jean-Paul Sartre, *Anti-Semite and Jew.* Translated by George J. Becker. New York: Schocken Books, 1948. Copyright © 1948 and renewed 1976.

Citadel Press/Kensington Publishing Corp. (www.kensingtonbooks.com) for Jean-Paul Sartre, *The Emotions: Outline of a Theory.* Translated by Bernard Frechtman. Secaucus, N.J.: Citadel Press, 1975.

Oxford University Press for Thomas Martin, "The Role of Emotion in Sartre's Portrait of the Anti-Semite," *Australasian Journal of Philosophy* 76, no. 2 (1998): 141–51.

Taylor & Francis (www.tandf.co.uk) for Thomas Martin, "Sartre, Sadism and Female Beauty Ideals," *Australian Feminist Studies* 11, no. 24 (1996): 243–52.

Introduction

The purpose of this book is twofold. First, it is intended to provide an introduction to the early period of Sartre's philosophical work through the pursuit of a theme: namely, what the Sartre of the 1930s and 1940s has to offer us in understanding oppression. Second, it is intended to support the claim that Sartre's early philosophy can indeed be useful in the study of oppression. In particular, I argue that Sartre's existentialism provides concepts (especially bad faith and other concepts emerging from his account of intersubjectivity) that can be useful tools in interpreting oppressive beliefs and behaviors such as those involved in racism and sexism.

Some readers of Sartrean existentialism have interpreted Sartre's account of the human condition as the depiction of the human subject as an individual, radically free consciousness that ought to be unaffected by its environment, history, and contact with others. In this picture the human subject appears to be disconnected from the world and others. Whatever else may be true of it, oppression involves intersubjectivity and relations with the world. The world itself does not oppress us, though facts about the world can make our lives difficult.[1] Other people oppress us, by acting in such a way as to illegitimately make us worse off than we would otherwise be. But this being "worse off" is not simply a matter of our relations with others (lack of respect, recognition, and so on). Oppression has material effects, involving access to institutions and resources. If we agree that oppression is founded on intersubjectivity and relations to the world (albeit of distorted or inauthentic kinds), a philosophy that does not take these features of human existence seriously seems unlikely to assist us in analyzing or understanding oppression. Hence, Sartrean existentialism, if that were how we were to interpret it, *would* be of little use in explaining social phenomena such as racism and sexism in which the force of circumstances and the behavior of others play paramount roles.

In opposition to this interpretation of Sartre, I argue for an alternative account of the Sartrean approach to human being, one in which the situatedness of freedom is stressed and through which the human condition is best understood as an ambiguous relation between free consciousness and facticity. From the standpoint of this account of human being as ambiguity, Sartre's concept of bad faith emerges as an account of attempts to resolve the ambiguity of human being by denying or ignoring one or another of the sides of the ambiguity. Bad faith is then seen as comprising two types: one in which transcendence is denied and facticity affirmed, the other in which facticity is denied in favor of a pure transcendence. This stands in contrast to commentaries on Sartre that tend to portray bad faith as being characterized only as a denial of transcendence.

I present two case studies in which the behavior and beliefs of an oppressor (in one case a racist anti-Semite, in the other a sexist who objectifies women) are investigated and interpreted in terms of bad faith. In these studies one or the other of the two types of bad faith is shown to be manifest. Furthermore the operation of bad faith is demonstrated to occur on three interrelated levels: the levels of the individual, one-to-one intersubjectivity, and the group or collective.

This study proceeds as follows. In chapter 1, Sartre's phenomenological ontology is examined. The examination considers Sartre's theory of consciousness and being. This culminates in an account of human reality (the fundamental condition of being human, which I also refer to as "the human condition") in which the subject emerges, not as transcendence, but rather as an ambiguous being living a tension between two realms of being: transcendence and facticity.

Because the main claim of this book is that oppressive beliefs and activities can be interpreted in terms of bad faith, it is imperative that we understand what bad faith amounts to and how it operates. Chapter 2 is devoted to an exploration of Sartre's concept of bad faith and is divided into two sections. The first section analyzes Sartre's concept of bad faith, interpreting it as an attempt to resolve, or a refusal of, the ambiguity that characterizes the human subject (as discussed in chapter 1). Interpreting bad faith as an attempt to escape ambiguity results in bad faith having two general types: the first characterized by a refusal of transcendence, the second by a refusal of facticity. Both types aim at simplifying or attenuating the complexity of human subjectivity (that is, denying the subject's position as a freedom in situation) though they do so by refusing different aspects of the ambiguity.

Having established the character of bad faith in the first section, in the second section I turn to an examination of Sartre's claim that bad faith is a matter of self-deception. How is self-deception possible for Sartre, who holds, contra Freud, that consciousness is undivided and translucent? If bad faith does require self-deception, and if we are to argue that bad faith can be involved in the all-too-real phenomenon of oppression, we must be able to demonstrate that it is possible. In order to demonstrate the possibility of self-deception in bad faith, in a way consistent with Sartre's model of consciousness, an appeal is made to Gestalt principles. The possibility of self-deception is then seen as arising from figure-ground differential focusing.

In chapter 3 I examine an example of oppression—racism—and seek to demonstrate the importance of using the concept of bad faith in understanding racist worldviews. The example is taken from Sartre's portrait of the anti-Semite in *Anti-Semite and Jew*.[2] My analysis identifies the beliefs and behavior of Sartre's anti-Semite as being based primarily on the type of bad faith characterized by a refusal of transcendence. I also discuss Sartre's theory of emotion and integrate elements of this theory into my analysis of the racist, highlighting the role of consciousness in partially constituting reality.

Oppression involves relations with others, including those who are the object of the oppression and others who act with the oppressor and assist in the creation of a social milieu that allows oppression. In chapter 4 the analysis of oppression and the human condition is shifted from the level of the individual to the level of intersubjectivity and group activity. It begins by examining the ontological bases of

Sartre's account of intersubjectivity, showing how one can objectify (or be objectified by) others. The significance of intersubjectivity and the effect of others with respect to the situating of the free self are discussed before moving on to a consideration of concrete relations with others. Intersubjectivity creates a subject/object dynamic through which the ambiguity of the self is made evident. Not surprisingly, then, contact with an other can result in the self's adoption of bad faith: the self refuses the ambiguity that intersubjectivity has highlighted. Sartre's approach to relations with others on the level of the group is then discussed and criticized. Finally, I return to the case of the anti-Semite (discussed in chapter 3), enriching the earlier analysis through the integration of elements of the discussion of intersubjectivity, and providing an interpretation of racism on the level of sociality.

In chapter 5 I discuss another example of oppression—a specific variety of sexism—and interpret this case as involving bad faith. However, in contrast to the scenario discussed in chapter 3, where the bad faith is based on refusal of transcendence, the bad faith involved in this example of oppression is of the type characterized by the sexist's refusal of facticity and situatedness, in favor of pure transcendence. I draw parallels between the sexist's position in a society that places emphasis on the appearance of women's bodies and the position of the sadist in sadism, which is one of the concrete relations with others discussed in the previous chapter. The social element of this phenomenon is captured through the framing of the analysis in terms of collective activity.

Before continuing, two limitations to this study must be made explicit. The first concerns the term *oppression* that appears in the title. Any full account of an oppression (a racism or a sexism, for example) will need to encompass systematic and structural features of a society that serve to constrain or harm some of its members. It has been claimed that these features may perform certain functions and serve particular interests, not as the result of the intentions of any individual or group, but through modes of discourse that contain and maintain norms and habits of representation, rules, and expectations, which are not under the control of any individual.[3] My interest in oppression in the context of this book does center on individuals, their intentions, and resulting complicity in oppression, with little focus on the structural features of oppression. As such, the account presented here can only hope to be a partial one. Partial though it may be, I believe it is still important. There are people who hold racist and sexist beliefs that they act on to the detriment of others. I maintain that these beliefs are not simply imposed (if they were, how could we explain the existence of anti-Apartheid whites in pre-1994 South Africa, male supporters of feminism in patriarchal societies, and so on?) but actively taken up. The project of understanding the worldviews, crises, and motivations of those who adopt such beliefs is an important and worthwhile one.

The second limitation to this study concerns the works of Sartre that are examined. They all fall within the early period of his career. Clearly, with respect to the first purpose of this book (to provide an introduction to the early Sartre) my choice of material makes sense. With respect to the second purpose (providing an account of what Sartre has to offer the study of oppression) the choice of material is more problematic. Sartre did go on to develop his ideas on the position of the individual in society (in his *Critique of Dialectical Reason*, for example) in respects that have an impact on our understanding of oppression (particularly the structural aspects of oppression).[4] However, given the limited focus with respect to oppression mentioned above, the works selected provide plenty of material for (at least a first step in) the pursuit of the project.

NOTES

1. As Simone de Beauvoir claims, "a situation of oppression . . . is never natural: man is never oppressed by things. . . . Only man can be an enemy of man." *Ethics of Ambiguity*, 81–82.

2. Sartre, *Anti-Semite and Jew*.

3. See, for example, Iris Marion Young, *Justice and the Politics of Difference*, chapter 2.

4. Sartre, *Critique of Dialectical Reason*.

1

Consciousness, the World, and Human Being

The main claim of this book is that some cases of oppression can be understood in terms of the oppressor engaging in bad faith and inauthentic relations with others, both of which involve refusals to recognize the nature of human being. The aim of this chapter is to present an account of Sartre's theory of consciousness, his phenomenological ontology, and the picture of human reality (that is, the defining condition of being human) that emerges from these. As a phenomenologist, Sartre's interest is in *phenomena*: the world as it appears to consciousness. Hence an understanding of Sartre's theory of consciousness (what consciousness is, to the extent that it *is* anything at all, and the relationship between consciousness and the world) is crucial to an understanding of the rest of his philosophy, including his accounts of freedom and human reality. Sartre's ontology relies heavily on his theory of consciousness. From his ontology and theory of consciousness emerges an account of human reality. In opposition to readings of Sartre that maintain that his account of human reality presents "man" as unbridled transcendence, I argue for an alternative interpretation in which human reality is understood as involving an ambiguous relation between freedom and situatedness in the world. This account of human reality will play a crucial role in the following chapters as it is this (or, rather, problems associated with such a human condition) that can provide the motivation for, and some explanation of, the various cases of oppression that later chapters address. Let us begin by considering Sartre's theory of consciousness.

CONSCIOUSNESS AND INTENTIONALITY

We have all believed that the spidery mind trapped things in its web, covered them with a white spit and slowly swallowed them, reducing them to its own substance. What is a table, a rock, a house? A certain assemblage of "contents of consciousness," a class of such contents. O digestive philosophy![1]

Against the "digestive philosophy," of which he accuses both idealism and Cartesian realism, Sartre, following Husserl, proposes that consciousness is *intentional*.[2] Intentionality refers to the way in which consciousness is directed toward (or intends) its object. "All consciousness . . . is consciousness *of* something."[3] As intentional, consciousness always posits an object, and thus, consciousness is directed outward and *contains* nothing, though it would be incorrect to say that it is empty. "Consciousness is neither empty nor full; it is neither to be filled nor to be emptied; it is purely and simply consciousness of the object."[4] Elsewhere Sartre describes consciousness as "clear as a strong wind."[5] Furthermore, "all consciousness is positional in that it transcends itself in order to reach an object, and it exhausts itself in this same positing."[6] So, for Sartre, consciousness is not some *thing* that contains ideas or representations. Consciousness is a relation to things out there in the world and *contains* nothing. However, this is not to say that consciousness is at the mercy of the world. It is true that consciousness does, in some respects, rely on its object. If all consciousness is consciousness of something, there clearly must be something in order for there to be consciousness. But consciousness is not a passive relation to the object; it is a constituting activity, which reveals its object.

Sartre's account of consciousness and its relationship to the world adopts an interesting position with respect to idealism and realism. At times Sartre appears to be a realist, at others an idealist. But how is this possible? If we take idealism, of whatever form, to be the claim that the world is dependent on consciousness, and realism, of whatever form, to be the claim that the world is independent of consciousness, there would appear to be no space between them, no middle ground. However, one finds both realist and idealist elements in Sartre's work. Let us examine first the realist aspect of Sartre's account.

Sartre's interpretation of intentionality reveals his realism. He writes:

> All consciousness is consciousness *of* something. This definition of consciousness can be taken in two very distinct senses: either we understand by this that consciousness is constitutive of the being of its object, or it means that consciousness in its inmost nature is a relation to a transcendent being. But the first interpretation of the formula destroys itself. (xxxvi)

"Consciousness is born *supported* by a being which is not itself" (xxxvii), and so consciousness cannot be the source of that being. The world is really out there and it does not depend on consciousness for its existence. On the contrary, the reverse is true. It is consciousness that depends on the world for its existence.

The type of realism employed by Sartre can be termed *direct realism*, as opposed to the *indirect realism* of Descartes.[7] Descartes holds that the world exists and that we have indirect access to it via ideas.[8] This is an example of the "digestive philosophy" that Sartre claims is disrupted by the intentionality of consciousness. Fell writes in the introduction to his translation of Sartre's essay on intentionality: "[Cartesian] realism and idealism alike had been guilty in effect of an often unexpressed correspondence theory which made mental surrogates for the real the only reality available to man."[9] Sartre holds that the world exists and that, contra Descartes, we have direct access to it. For example, Sartre claims: "You see this tree, to be sure. But you see it just where it is: at the side of the road, in the midst of the dust, alone and writhing in the heat."[10] Our contact with the tree is not indirect, via a representation of it "in our heads." Rather, we have direct contact with the tree where it stands in the world.

Despite the evident realism in Sartre's thought, one also finds elements that can appear idealist, in that they seem to give consciousness a role in constituting the world. Consciousness brings to the world qualities based on negations or *nothingnesses*. We have already come across one such negation: consciousness is consciousness of something other than itself. That is, in being conscious of X, consciousness is *not* X. In this way, consciousness *transcends* its object. Another way in which being conscious of an object involves negation is that positing a particular object, focusing on it rather than the other things that surround it, involves excluding it from the rest of the world. So, in being conscious of X, X is not just not consciousness, it is also *not* any other thing. Importantly, for Sartre, negations do not exist in the world independently of consciousness. Consciousness brings nothingness to the world.

Nothingnesses, however, include more than the simple negations we have just mentioned. Evaluative judgments involve nothingness. Values involve descriptions of the way one wishes the world to be, or how one would wish oneself to act in a hypothetical situation, and so are precisely descriptions of the way the world is *not*. It might be objected that, surely, we sometimes value things that we do have: friends, possessions, and so on. However, valuing those things carries with it the desire that we should continue to have them or would like to have more of them, and this is not the way the world actually is at the moment. Because it is a nothingness, a value must be brought to the world by consciousness. For Sartre, any quality of the world that relies on some notion of the way things might be, but are not now, is a nothingness. An example of this is his account of fragility and destruction.

> A being is fragile if it carries in its being a definite possibility of nonbeing . . . [and] it is through man that fragility comes into being. . . . It is man who renders cities destructible, precisely because he posits them as fragile and as precious and because he adopts a system of protective measures with regard to them. . . . It is necessary then to recognize that destruction is an essentially human thing and that *it is man* who destroys his cities through the agency of earthquakes or directly, who destroys his ships through cyclones or directly.[11]

Sartre's claim is that there are aspects of the world, as we experience it, that are mind-dependent. He is not, in the case of destruction, for example, denying that there can be rearrangements of matter brought about by events such as earthquakes that can occur regardless of whether there is anyone there to witness them. But the quality of *de-*

struction is mind-dependent. It is only in relation to someone with certain concerns that a rearrangement of matter counts as destruction rather than as, say, creation or indeed something of no interest at all.

Absences, too, are nothingnesses brought to the world by consciousness (9–10). For example, when I arrive home from work I am usually greeted by my dog. Occasionally, however, the dog runs off to play with one of her friends, and on those days I get home and see that she is not there. I experience her absence. We might be tempted to say that her absence from the yard is just a fact about the material world (like the rearrangement of the vase's matter, as opposed to its being broken, is a fact about the vase I have dropped), which, while requiring consciousness to notice it, does not require consciousness to provide it. In other words, we might ask: "Is the dog's absence really a mind-dependent nothingness?" It is true that the dog really is not there, though neither is there a warthog nor a steam engine in the yard. Yet I do not experience the absence of a warthog or a steam engine, because I do not expect to see them. I experience the absence of the dog (perhaps even more vividly than I experience the presence of the coral tree) because I expect her to be there. Her *notable* absence, which is a key element in my perceptual field, is as it is in relation to me and my expectations, and so is mind-dependent.

Mind-dependent qualities of the world (the broken vase, the absent dog) are experienced precisely as qualities of the world. However, this does not contradict Sartre's realism, as "the world" in this case refers to the human world, the world as the site of subjectivity. Remember that Sartre is a phenomenologist. He is interested in describing the world as it appears. There are aspects of the world as it appears that include such things as possible courses of action, instruments, and evaluated objects. Such things are necessarily dependent upon consciousness, not for their brute existence, but for their existence as things with human-related aspects. The theme of mind-dependent elements of our world will be revisited in chapter 3, in the course of a discussion on emotion, where the focus will be on the capacity of consciousness to "color" the world, endowing objects "out there" with qualities such as hatefulness and lovability.

Sartre's approach to intentionality plays an important role in understanding the nature of human existence, in which one is both a part of the world and separated from it. To the extent that I am conscious of things "out there," my consciousness relies on those things and their being out there in the world, and thus I am fundamentally related to the world. But to the extent that I am *conscious* of those things, there is a distance between the world and me. This ambiguous condition of both being a part of the world and yet separate from it will be found, later in this chapter, to be definitive of human reality. However, it will first be necessary to examine further elements of Sartre's theory of consciousness. In particular, the different modes of consciousness that Sartre postulates will provide necessary background to understanding the being of conscious, human being and its relation to the world and itself, which will in turn form the basis of an account of human reality.

MODES OF CONSCIOUSNESS

Positional and Non-Positional Consciousness

It has already been said that consciousness, as consciousness *of* something, is always directed toward, or "posits," an object. But, for Sartre, the positing of an object is not all there is to consciousness, for consciousness must be conscious of itself as consciousness.

> This is a necessary condition, for if my consciousness were not consciousness of being consciousness of the table, it would then be consciousness of that table without consciousness of being so. In other words, it would be a consciousness ignorant of itself, an unconscious— which is absurd. (xxviii)

Why must consciousness be conscious of itself as being consciousness of its object? Sartre seems to view this as self-evident and does little to support this assumption. However, I take it that something like the following may provide an explanation of this point, as well as give some content to Sartre's idea of negation. If its object purely took up consciousness, the negating role of consciousness would be impossible. Consciousness of the object would simply become "object." It is unclear how there could even be an object, as figure against background, without the negating activity of consciousness. It is also part and parcel of the intentionality of consciousness that it be conscious of an object other than itself. Intentionality is a *relation* to an object, and so it must be *between* something and something else. In order for consciousness to be consciousness of an object other than itself there must be some sort of awareness of self in opposition to awareness of the object.

The claim that consciousness must be conscious of itself may appear to run into the difficulty of requiring an infinite regress. If all consciousness must be conscious of itself, then in order for me to be conscious of the table, I must be conscious of my consciousness of the table. However, would that not in turn require that I must be conscious of my consciousness of my consciousness of the table, in which case I must also be conscious of my consciousness of my consciousness of my consciousness of the table, and so on? We are left, it would appear, with two choices. We could stop at one of the terms in the series, in which case we must be willing to accept a non-self-conscious final term. For Sartre, such a result is out of the question. As we have seen, he claims that the idea of a "consciousness ignorant of itself, an unconscious" is "absurd" (xxviii). The alternative would be to refuse to allow a non-self-conscious final term, in which case we are left with an infinite regress, which is also "absurd" (xxviii).[12]

So, what are we to do? Sartre deals with the problem by claiming that the consciousness of an object and the consciousness of consciousness of an object are two different modes of consciousness. "If we wish to avoid an infinite regress, there must be an immediate, *non-cognitive* relation of the self to itself" (xxviii–xxix; emphasis added). To this "non-cognitive relation of the self to itself" Sartre gives the name *non-positional* (or, sometimes, *non-thetic*) consciousness, which he contrasts with *positional* (or *thetic*) consciousness. We have seen that consciousness, as intentional, must intend an object. Positional consciousness intends, or posits, an object other than itself. It is consciousness *of* an object. However, intentionality also requires that consciousness be aware of itself as consciousness of an object. This non-positional self-awareness is consciousness of consciousness, but it does not posit consciousness as an object. Consciousness is not an object and cannot be so posited. Sartre writes:

The immediate consciousness which I have of perceiving does not permit me either to judge or to will or to be ashamed. It does not *know* my perception, does not *posit* it; all that there is of intention in my actual consciousness is directed toward the outside, toward the world. In other words, every positional consciousness of an object is at the same time a non-positional consciousness of itself. (xxix)

Often, to distinguish non-positional consciousness of consciousness from positional consciousness of an object, Sartre puts parentheses around the "of" in the former. So, for example, there is positional consciousness of the table that is also non-positional consciousness (of) itself (xxx).

Sartre's postulation of non-positional self-awareness is intended to escape the problem of an infinite regress. While positional consciousness must be conscious (of) itself, non-positional self-consciousness is of a different nature to the positional. There is no requirement for consciousness of or (of) non-positional consciousness. As non-positional, this self-consciousness does not intend an object; it is not itself intentional, despite being a crucial component of intentionality.

A further consequence of the non-positional self-awareness that, for Sartre, accompanies all conscious acts (be they pre-reflective or reflective, a distinction I will discuss in the next section) is that consciousness is *translucent* (49). In claiming that consciousness is translucent, Sartre sets his theory of consciousness in opposition to those that would claim an *opaque* subject or, like Freud, an unconscious. Consciousness is aware not only of its object but also of itself as consciousness of the object. Thus consciousness is open to itself, unable to be unaware of itself as consciousness of its object. The translucency of consciousness will figure significantly when, in chapter 2, we come to consider the possibility of bad faith as a case of self-deception.

The two modes of consciousness, positional and non-positional, which have been examined so far, should not be considered as separate acts of consciousness. Rather, they are components of the same conscious act of intending an object. Sartre writes:

We understand now why the first consciousness of consciousness is not positional; it is because it is one with the consciousness of which it is consciousness. At one stroke it determines itself as consciousness of perception and as perception. . . . This self-consciousness we ought to consider not as a new consciousness, but as *the only mode of existence which is possible for a consciousness of something.* (xxx)

Thus we have positional and non-positional consciousness as two necessary aspects of any conscious act. All consciousness is a positional consciousness of an object and is simultaneously non-positionally conscious (of) itself.

Pre-Reflective and Reflective Consciousness

Apart from the positional and non-positional modes of consciousness, Sartre also refers to pre-reflective and reflective consciousness. While all consciousness is accompanied by non-positional self-consciousness, this non-positional self-consciousness should not be confused with reflection. Sartre takes it that consciousness is typically *pre-reflective*, meaning that it is directed at some object in the world other than itself. Although pre-reflective consciousness of an object is accompanied by non-positional self-consciousness, this self-consciousness does not introduce an *I* as the object (or part of the object) posited. It simply makes its contribution to the intentionality of the conscious act by making the object *not-I*. Sartre gives the following example:

> When I run after a streetcar, when I look at the time, when I am absorbed in contemplating a portrait there is no *I*. There is consciousness *of the streetcar-having-to-be-overtaken*, etc., and non-positional consciousness of consciousness. In fact, I am then plunged into the world of objects; it is they which constitute the unity of my consciousnesses; it is they which present themselves with values, with attractive and repellent qualities—but *me*, I have disappeared; I have annihilated myself. There is no place for *me* on this level.[13]

While Sartre gives primacy to pre-reflective consciousness and engagement with the world, consciousness can be reflective. He claims: "Reflection is the for-itself [that is, conscious being] conscious *of* itself."[14] Thus reflective consciousness is a positional consciousness that takes consciousness as its object. However, as has already been said, consciousness, as an intentional relation to an object, is not itself

an object. How then can there be positional consciousness of consciousness? There are two ways in which consciousness can posit itself. First, consciousness can posit some past act of itself. Consciousness can reflect on what it has been before: on memories, past
emotions, and projects. Second, consciousness can posit an *I* in the
midst of activity. While my running after a streetcar might most typically
be a matter of pre-reflective consciousness of "the-streetcar-having-to-
be-overtaken," I can be aware of myself running after the streetcar,
and not simply in the non-positional mode of self-awareness. For instance, I might think to myself "Here I am again having to run to catch
the streetcar. I really must leave the house a little earlier in future."
Sartre describes this type of reflection as follows:

> There is an unreflected act of reflection, without an *I*, which is directed
> on a reflected consciousness. The latter becomes the object of the re-
> flecting consciousness without ceasing to affirm its own object (a chair,
> a mathematical truth, etc.). At the same time a new object appears
> which is the occasion for an affirmation by reflective consciousness, and
> which is consequently not on the same level as the unreflected con-
> sciousness (because the latter consciousness is an absolute which has
> no need of reflective consciousness in order to exist) nor on the same
> level as the object of the reflected consciousness (chair, etc.). This tran-
> scendent object of the reflective act is the *I*.[15]

This passage is an interesting one, for it not only speaks of the possibility of reflection, but also of the limits of reflection. While consciousness
can reflect on its past acts and, in a sense, witness itself in action, it is
also the case that consciousness cannot grasp itself. As Sartre here
claims, the *I* posited by reflective consciousness is a "transcendent object." It will be recalled that the key aspect of the intentionality of consciousness is that consciousness posits an object *that is not itself*. The
same is true for reflective consciousness. Just as with pre-reflective consciousness, reflective consciousness involves a non-positional self-
awareness that causes a break between consciousness and its object. In
the case of reflective consciousness, consciousness is the object of
consciousness, but *the consciousness reflecting and the consciousness
reflected upon are not identical*. Otherwise, Sartre writes, we would

have to accept the existence of "the phantom dyad 'the-reflection-reflecting.'"[16] Rather, "to the extent that reflection is *knowledge*, the reflected-on must necessarily be the *object* for the reflective; and this implies a separation of being" (151). While consciousness can be reflective, the object of the reflection and the intending consciousness are not the same and, thus, consciousness always misses itself.

Although the intentionality of reflection causes a break between the reflective and the reflected-on, there is, nonetheless, a "bond of being" between the two. Otherwise, as Sartre writes:

> Reflective knowledge, and in particular the *cogito* would lose their certainty and would obtain in exchange only a certain probability, scarcely definable. It is agreed then that reflection must be united to that which is reflected-on by a bond of being, that the reflective consciousness must be the consciousness reflected-on. (151)

Hence, there is a sense in which "the reflective is the reflected-on" (155). For this reason the reflected-on acts as an unusual type of object, a *quasi-object*, for the reflecting consciousness. "The reflective is the reflected-on in complete immanence although in the form of 'not-being-in-itself.' It is this which well demonstrates the fact that the reflected-on is not wholly an object but a quasi-object for reflection" (155). The "quasi-objectness" of the reflected-on refers not so much to the insubstantiality of consciousness (for, as we will see later, past acts of consciousness form part of one's situation and a ground for future acts), but rather to the lesser "distance" between the reflective and the reflected-on, compared with, say, the "distance" between consciousness and a table. Reflective consciousness has an intimate, close proximity to its object. However, while the reflective and the reflected-on must be united by a bond of being, "there can be no question . . . of a total identification of the reflective and the reflected-on" (151). Sartre concludes that "it is necessary that the reflective simultaneously be and not be the reflected-on" (151). As we will see in the next section, Sartre claims that a similarly (though not identically) ambiguous structure is definitive of being-for-itself, the being of consciousness.[17]

PHENOMENOLOGICAL ONTOLOGY AND HUMAN REALITY

Sartre's notion of intentionality and his distinctions between positional and non-positional consciousness and between pre-reflective and reflective consciousness support a further distinction that he makes between being-for-itself and being-in-itself. It is this latter distinction that we will now examine as it is through this distinction that the account of freedom and human reality will emerge.

Sartre holds that there are "two radically separated regions of being," being-in-itself and being-for-itself.[18] Being-for-itself is the mode of conscious being, the being of humans in their capacity as subjects. Before examining being-for-itself we will examine the other major mode of being, being-in-itself, to which being-for-itself stands in contrast.

Being-In-Itself

Being-in-itself is typically understood to be the mode of being of non-conscious objects. While it is certainly the case that non-conscious objects do exist in the mode of being-in-itself, beings-in-themselves include much more than tables, rocks, hubcaps, and the like. Being-in-itself is best understood as a mode of being (that is, a manner of existing) in which a being is identical with itself. Sartre asks, "Is this not precisely the definition of the in-itself—or if you prefer—the principle of identity?" (58) and Thomas Busch argues that "throughout *Being and Nothingness* the most persistent characterization of being-in-itself is that of *identity*."[19]

Sartre aligns the "principle of identity" with the "principle of analytical judgment" through which A is A.[20] Being-in-itself, under the governance of the principle of identity, is self-identical, self-contained, "it does not enter into any connection with what is not itself" (xlii). Being-in-itself simply "is what it is" and "is never anything but what it is" (xlii). Tables, rocks, and hubcaps are clearly beings-in-themselves, they simply are what they are. But so too is the past of consciousness, which "is a for-itself fixed in in-itself" (202). The ego (which, for Sartre, is the object of reflection rather than the self) also exists in the mode of being-in-itself. Consciousness can objectify the consciousness of another, giving it being-for-others, which fixes that consciousness, giving it the "character of the in-itself" (266).[21] Thus we can see that while it is true that being-in-itself is the being of objects, *object* is broadly defined in the work of Sartre to include objectified consciousness (such as past consciousness, the ego, and the consciousness of another) as well as simple material objects.

In speaking of being-in-itself as the being of objects, the issue of the relationship between the in-itself and consciousness is raised. In calling an in-itself an object we could mean two things. First, the in-itself is an object of consciousness. Second, and alternatively, the in-itself has transcendent existence and, while it is a potential object of consciousness, it need not actually be an object of consciousness in order for it to participate in the mode of being of the in-itself. These possibilities take us back to what was said earlier in this chapter about Sartre's position with respect to realism and idealism. It will be recalled that Sartre is a realist in that he holds that the world exists independently of consciousness. But does the world have the character of the in-itself independent of consciousness? Recall that Sartre holds that rather than the world depending on consciousness, it is consciousness that depends on the world for its existence. So, when Sartre claims that there is an "ontological primacy of the in-itself over the for-itself" (619), we can see that the in-itself is, indeed, independent of consciousness. The in-itself exists independently of our perception of it and, therefore, need not be an object of consciousness.

However, this realism is complicated by the idealist elements of Sartre's thought. Consciousness perceives objects, rather than undifferentiated being and, as we saw earlier, it is consciousness that splits apart being, transforming it into a world of discrete things. While this splitting apart of being does not effect being itself, it is constitutive of the human life-world. Furthermore, there are affective properties of beings-in-themselves that are given by consciousness, though these properties are experienced as transcending the subject, that is, as belonging to the object rather than the perceiver. While it might be tempting to put the role of consciousness with respect to the in-itself down to illusion, the phenomenological nature of Sartre's enterprise precludes such dismissal. As an existential phenomenologist, Sartre is concerned to describe the phenomena of our world, and the aspects of our world that have their origins in subjectivity must be taken seriously. In summary, the answer to the question "Is it necessary for being-in-itself that the in-itself be an object of consciousness?" is in the negative, with the qualification that there are aspects of the in-itself *as experienced* that have their origin in consciousness.

Being-For-Itself

Being-for-itself is conscious being. As we have already seen, consciousness depends on being, as there must be something that it reveals, something *of* which it is conscious. This being upon which consciousness depends exists, as an intentional object, in the mode of being-in-itself. However, consciousness also depends on being in another way. Consciousness is an activity of *a* being, and this being is what Sartre terms a being-for-itself. As we saw earlier, for Sartre, consciousness is not a thing; it is a relation. And we can now see what consciousness is a relation between; it is a relation between an object (posited by consciousness) and the being that bears consciousness (being-for-itself). Clearly, consciousness and being-for-itself are not identical, but nor are they separate existences; being-for-itself must be conscious, and consciousness must be an activity of a being. But consciousness, though connected to being-for-itself, is not itself a being. Consciousness as an intentional activity is a nihilation of being, an introduction of nothingness to the world, and it is doubly dependent on being, in that it, first, must have an object to intend and, second, must be an activity of a being.

While Sartre often uses the terms *consciousness* and *being-for-itself* interchangeably, he does so metonymically. Hazel Barnes provides the following account of the relationship between consciousness and being:

> Although consciousness reveals being, the fundamental opposition on which [Sartre] builds his ontology is not that between consciousness and being but the distinction between two regions of being, only one of which is characterized as inextricably associated with consciousness. These are being-in-itself and being-for-itself, but insofar as being-for-itself *is*, it has the same being as being-in-itself. It is distinguished only by the presence in itself of the active negating activity we experience as consciousness. Thus the two regions of being are inseparable except abstractly, and the truth is that the distinction between being-in-itself and being-for-itself is less clear cut and more complex than first appears.[22]

Sartre sometimes uses *being-for-itself* to refer to consciousness itself, sometimes to refer to conscious being. For example: "The For-itself and the In-itself are reunited by a synthetic connection which is nothing other than the For-itself itself."[23] Here Sartre's first use of the term *for-itself* refers to being-for-itself as consciousness, that intentional activity that splits apart being and separates itself from being-in-itself. His second use of the term, however, refers to being-for-itself in the wider sense of conscious being, in which one finds a connection between consciousness and being.

Sartre's theory of consciousness plays a crucial role in his account of human reality, as it is through his theory of consciousness that Sartre establishes that beings-for-themselves are free. Sartre holds that we are always, in all circumstances, radically free. As conscious being, being-for-itself is free because consciousness, as a negating activity, introduces nothingness into the world. Being-for-itself is that being through which this nothingness is introduced. The nothingness with which consciousness encases its objects (by intending them, evaluating them, and so on) separates being-for-itself from the world of cause and effect, thus removing being-for-itself from determination and giving it radical freedom (435–36).

Sartre describes the reflective consciousness of freedom as *anguish*.[24] The for-itself's reflection on its freedom is anguished because through such reflection the for-itself realizes that there is nothing to compel it to act in any particular way. Thus the for-itself bears responsibility for what it will do. The future is open and no past act or state of affairs can fully determine a future act. Sartre describes anguish in the face of both the future and the past. With respect to the future he writes:

> In establishing a certain conduct as a possibility and precisely because it is *my* possibility, I am aware that *nothing* can compel me to adopt that conduct. Yet I am indeed already there in the future; it is for the sake of that being which I will be there at the turning of the path that I now exert all my strength, and in this sense there is already a relation between my future being and my present being. But a nothingness has slipped into the heart of this relation; I *am* not the self which I will be. . . . Anguish is precisely my consciousness of being my own future, in the mode of not-being.[25]

., nothing compels me to act in any particular way in the future. While there is a bond of being between me in the present and me in the future, this relation is not determining.

With respect to anguish in the face of the past, Sartre writes of a gambler who has

> freely and sincerely decided not to gamble any more and who when he approaches the gaming table, suddenly sees all his resolutions melt away. . . . The earlier resolution of "not playing any more" is always *there*, and in the majority of cases the gambler when in the presence of the gaming table, turns toward it as if to ask for help. . . . But what he apprehends then in anguish is precisely the total inefficacy of the past resolution. . . . The resolution is still *me* to the extent that I realize constantly my identity with myself across the temporal flux, but it is no longer *me*— due to the fact that it has become an object *for* my consciousness. . . . The resolution is there still, I *am* it in the mode of not-being. (32–33)

Thus, the past cannot determine our future behavior. What we were, we are no longer, and we are not able to absolve ourselves of responsibility for our future acts through appeals to the past.

Sartre takes it that awareness of freedom is an ever-present aspect of us. We might agree with him that we do seem to be free, and yet ask: "Are we *really* free?" Even the committed determinist can accept that we *feel* free, though she will deny that we actually *are* free. Regarding the possibility of determinism, Sartre writes:

> It would be vain to object that the sole condition of this anguish is ignorance of the underlying physiological determinism. According to such a view my anxiety would come from lack of knowing the real and effective incentives which in the darkness of the unconscious determine my action. In reply we shall point out . . . that anguish has not appeared to us as a *proof* of human freedom. . . . We wished only to show that there exists a specific consciousness of freedom, and we wished to show that this consciousness is anguish. . . . Now *from this point of view the existence of a physiological determinism could not invalidate the results of our description.* (33; emphasis added)

In other words, while determinism is a metaphysical possibility, Sartre, as a phenomenologist trying to describe human reality, maintains that he is right to include freedom as a crucial element in that description. Could freedom be an illusion? Perhaps, but it if it is an illusion it is a definitive and indispensable one. As Sartre writes, "this determinism, a reflective defense against anguish, is not given as a reflective *intuition*. It avails nothing against the *evidence* of freedom" (40). Sartre takes it that we constantly experience ourselves as facing choices ("the *evidence* of freedom") and so any description of how things are for us must include reference to freedom.[26]

In Sartre's descriptions of anguish in the face of the future and the past we are reminded of what was said earlier about reflective consciousness: that the consciousness reflecting and the consciousness reflected upon are not identical. While there remains a "bond of being" between me as reflector and the past or future me as reflected-on, they are not identical. There remains a break in being between the two. It is by virtue of this break in being that the for-itself is free (as the break disallows determination) and anguish is the realization of that break.

Being-for-itself is conscious and free, and connected to this is being-for-itself's lack of fixed identity. Being-in-itself, we saw, is governed by the principle of identity, that is, it simply is what it is. Being-in-itself is determined by its former states and, under the principle of identity, is no more than those states. It is locked in by, and completely taken up with, itself. This is not the case with being-for-itself. The break in being between the self reflecting and the self reflected-on translates to a break between the self and its possibilities. Being-for-itself is not identical with itself. Conscious being, as an activity, a movement of change, does not exhibit the self-identity manifest in being-in-itself, and thus being-for-itself is not governed by the principle of identity.

While "being-in-itself *is* what it is," being-for-itself "*has to be* what it is."[27] Another way of putting this is to say that being-for-itself must *become* what it is. The reason for this is that being-for-itself is a perpetual flight from presence into the future (125).[28] That toward which being-for-itself directs itself is its project of becoming, in the light of which the world is interpreted, but there is no final resting place. As a *perpetual* flight into the future, a continual striving, being-for-itself, once having reached a point, is already beyond it. Whatever being-for-itself is at any particular time is a manifestation of its free spontaneity. Being-for-itself is continually creating itself, continually moving toward endless possibilities.

Although being-for-itself chooses itself, it never actually *is* what it chooses. Sartre writes of being-for-itself that it "is a being which is what it is not and which is not what it is" (79). This seemingly paradoxical statement can be understood as follows. Although, by virtue of consciousness, being-for-itself is free and future directed, it is still a being and so does exist; after all, consciousness is an activity of a being. So being-for-itself is. But as a free flight toward the future (necessitated by its being conscious being), being-for-itself has gone beyond what it now is. Thus we can interpret the statement "being-for-itself is what it is not and is not what it is" as meaning that being-for-itself is (as a flight toward the future) what it is not (yet), and is not (yet) what it is (now).[29]

However, having said all this, being-for-itself is not simply an utterly unconstrained movement toward the future, although, as we will see in the next section, Sartre is often taken to mean just this. Being-for-itself is not disconnected from the world. Earlier we saw Barnes claim that "insofar as being-for-itself is, it has the same being as being-in-itself."[30] We should also keep in mind that Sartre has told us that being-for-itself and being-in-itself are connected in being-for-itself itself. There are aspects of being-for-itself that are object-like, which are governed by the principle of identity; in short, there are aspects of being-for-itself that partake of being-in-itself. These object-like aspects of being-for-itself Sartre collectively terms *facticity*.[31] One's facticity includes such things as one's history, gender, race, nationality, class, bodily particularities, and so on. In short, facticity is the facts about one. While facticity consists of facts about being-for-itself, being-for-itself *transcends* its facticity: that is, it has freedom with respect to its interpretation or evaluation of its facticity. The meaning being-for-itself gives to its history, gender, race, and so on, the place that they hold and the role that they play in its current projects, is, to a certain extent at least, up to being-for-itself. But the facts that make up facticity are there in the world and cannot be avoided or wished away. Being-for-itself has race, gender, and class. Those beings that have being-for-itself can choose to value their facticity in any number of ways, but cannot choose the very existence of their facticity. Similarly, being-for-itself's history, while it is the product of past choices, now is beyond its control, as those past acts are attached to it regardless of how those past acts are evaluated. As facticity is, in certain respects, beyond being-for-itself's control, being-for-itself is not the total foundation of what it is, and it is plagued by this contingency of its own being. Although facticity consists of givens concerning a person, and although they "are what they are" (in the mode of being-in-itself), Sartre stresses that they should not be understood to be determining of being-for-itself. Being-for-itself is free and is not *determined* by its facticity, though as we will see, it is *limited* by its facticity.

Transcendence, Facticity, and Human Reality

The issue of the capacity of being-for-itself to transcend its facticity is an interesting and controversial one within Sartrean scholarship. In claiming that being-for-itself can transcend its facticity, does this mean that facticity is (or should be) irrelevant to being-for-itself? Or can facticity constrain, delimit, or condition freedom? Should we understand human reality, as being-for-itself, to be simply transcending, as free consciousness, or does facticity play a more important role in human reality? This is an important issue because it deeply affects our understanding of human reality. As will become apparent, Sartre can seem inconsistent in his presentation of human reality, and two distinct interpretations of human reality emerge from *Being and Nothingness*. The first is that human reality is simply pure, unconditioned freedom as transcendence. The second is that human reality is transcendence *and* facticity, or, more precisely, that freedom is always situated such that transcendence and facticity are inseparable and that facticity, while not determining freedom, certainly does limit it, and must be seen as a crucial component of the human condition.[32] Let us now examine some of the evidence for each of these interpretations.[33]

In several places in *Being and Nothingness*, Sartre makes statements that seem to affirm the first interpretation of human reality, namely, that human reality is to be understood wholly as transcendent freedom. For example:

Man is free because he is not himself but presence to himself. The being which is what it is can not be free. . . . As we have seen, for human
reality, to be is to *choose oneself*; nothing comes to it either from the outside or from within which it can *receive or accept*. Without any help
whatsoever, it is entirely abandoned to the intolerable necessity of making itself be—down to the slightest detail. Thus freedom is not a being;
it is *the being* of man—i.e., his nothingness of being.[34]

Note here Sartre's claim that freedom (as transcendence) is *the* being
of man. There is no mention here of facticity as a central component
of human reality. This is not to say that Sartre is here denying the existence of human facticity, but he does seem to be playing down its
importance to human reality. Other passages that seem to diminish
the role of facticity include:

It is impossible for a determined process to act upon a spontaneity, exactly as it is impossible for objects to act upon consciousness. (442)

Either man is wholly determined (which is inadmissible, especially because a determined consciousness—i.e., a consciousness externally
motivated—becomes itself pure exteriority and ceases to be consciousness) or else man is wholly free. (442)

Each for-itself, in fact, is a for-itself only by choosing itself beyond nationality and race just as it speaks only by choosing the designation beyond the syntax and morphemes. This "beyond" is enough to assure its
total independence in relation to the structures which it surpasses. (520)

Through these passages "man" emerges as free, with "total independence" in relation to "his" facticity. It is from passages such as these
that many of Sartre's critics have developed a view of Sartrean "man"
as an utterly independent, transcendent freedom detached from "his"
environment.[35]

However, one also finds much in *Being and Nothingness* that af-
firms the importance of facticity to human reality. To begin with,
Sartre claims that without the "coefficient of adversity" provided by
being-in-itself, in the form of facticity and objects in the world, freedom would be impossible. He goes on to say:

Would it not be reasonable to say, along with certain contemporary
philosophers: if no obstacle, then no freedom? And as we can not admit

that freedom by itself creates its own obstacle—which would be absurd for anyone who has understood the meaning of spontaneity—there seems to be here a kind of ontological priority of the in-itself over the for-itself.[36]

Thus freedom requires connection to the world. At this juncture there can be little doubt in the mind of the reader of the importance of facticity to freedom. Further to this, Sartre claims that not only does facticity make freedom possible it also limits freedom:

It is nonetheless true that freedom encounters or seems to encounter limitations on account of the *given* which it surpasses or nihilates. To show that the coefficient of adversity of the thing and its character as an obstacle (joined to its character as an instrument) is indispensable to the existence of a freedom is to use an argument that cuts two ways; for while it enables us to establish that freedom is not invalidated by the given, it indicates, on the other hand, something like an ontological conditioning of freedom. (484)

Thus Sartre holds that freedom can be conditioned by the given. Facticity is both an essential and limiting factor for freedom. However, Sartre has also claimed that "freedom is not invalidated by the given." How is it that Sartre can maintain both that freedom is "total," and that it is conditioned by facticity? The key to understanding this lies in Sartre's negative interpretation of freedom.[37] He writes: "It is necessary to point out to 'common sense' that the formula 'to be free' does not mean 'to obtain what one has wished' but rather 'by oneself to determine oneself to wish' (in the broad sense of choosing). In other words success is not important to freedom."[38] To be free is to not be determined, as opposed to being free in the sense of being free to do, and this is why I refer to Sartre's interpretation of freedom as negative. Although being-for-itself is wholly undetermined, and thus absolutely free to choose, it is limited by its situation to a certain range of choices. One way to think of this through analogy is in terms of greater and lesser infinities. For example, the set of odd integers is an infinite one, though it is a lesser infinity than the set of integers (even and odd). Although the set of odd integers has infinite members, none of its members is even, because its members are limited to the terms of the set. Similarly, being free, any for-itself may have infinite possibilities within its situation, but its possibilities will all be limited to that situation.

By interpreting Sartre's concept of freedom in this way, sense can be made of such statements as "the slave in chains is as free as his master" (550) and that "there is no situation in which the for-itself would be *more free* than in others" (549). Both the slave and the master are free. There are, of course, significant differences between them in terms of what their respective situations will allow them to do. But this does not detract from the fact that they are not determined, no matter how oppressive or privileged their respective situations may be. Certainly, such a view of freedom, as it stands, is severely limited in terms of its usefulness to speaking of political freedom. When people speak of freedom in a politically significant sense, they are after much more than mere non-determination. But perhaps this is not Sartre's task here.[39] *Being and Nothingness* is concerned with elucidating a phenomenological ontology. This is not to say that Sartre had no interest in pursuing the issue of freedom in its politically valuable sense, and he spent much of his career after *Being and Nothingness* doing just that.

We are both free and conditioned. Human reality is an ambiguous relation between transcendence and facticity. The following passage underlines the ambiguous, dual nature of human reality:

> This inapprehensible *fact* of my condition [facticity] . . . is what causes the for-itself, while choosing the *meaning* of its situation and while constituting itself as the foundation of itself in situation, *not to choose* its position. This part of my condition is what causes me to apprehend myself simultaneously as totally responsible for my being—inasmuch as I am its foundation—and yet as totally unjustifiable. Without facticity consciousness could choose its attachments to the world in the same way as the souls in Plato's *Republic* choose their condition. I could determine myself to "be born a worker" or to "be born a bourgeois." But on the other hand facticity can not constitute me as *being* a bourgeois or *being* a worker.[40]

We are limited by our facticity, but not determined by it. However, we are not free in spite of our facticity; rather we are free because of it.

Thus there appear to be two possible interpretations of human reality, as presented in *Being and Nothingness*. The first is that human reality is transcendent freedom and that freedom is totally unconstrained. The second is that human reality is transcendence *and* facticity, whereby freedom is constrained (though not determined) by facticity. Which of these two interpretations should we adopt? Thomas Anderson makes a strong case for accepting that, on balance, Sartre himself favors the first interpretation in *Being and Nothingness*:

> In the final analysis, I believe that the freedom Sartre so emphasizes [in *Being and Nothingness*], a freedom which he designates as absolute, total, and infinite because it transcends and escapes one's facticity, no matter how repressive, and because it can confer all kinds of different meanings on that facticity, even if it can not change it, is only a freedom of consciousness. . . . I believe that this freedom is at most a freedom of consciousness, not the concrete freedom of a situated human being.[41]

However, despite Anderson's argument to the contrary, I will adopt the second interpretation throughout the current work. I have two main reasons for doing this. The first is that many of Sartre's more extreme statements regarding freedom, statements that may lend support to the first interpretation, can still be compatible with the second interpretation. Recall what was said earlier with respect to Sartre's (infamous) claim that "the slave in chains is as free as his master."[42] It was suggested that if one recognizes, first, that Sartre's concept of freedom is freedom as non-determination rather than freedom to do and, second, that freedom is limited by its situation, then sense could be made of Sartre's claim. Also, given this interpretation, Sartre should not be viewed as denying that the slave is oppressed. In saying that the slave is free, Sartre confers upon the slave ontological freedom only. It is another question if the situation and conditions of action that the slave faces are adequate, such that the slave's practical freedom is valuable, and it is within the purview of Sartre's theory to maintain that they are not. It is nonetheless true that Sartre often leaves himself open to being interpreted as holding that "man" is an abstract freedom. On this issue, and in support of the interpretation of human reality as transcendence and facticity, Linda Bell writes:

> Sartre himself is prone to overstatement in many of his claims about freedom, sometimes seeming to ignore or reject important qualifications he at other times is so careful to enunciate. Although Sartre thus bears some responsibility for many of the most common misconceptions of his view of freedom, the extent to which he explicitly argued against these, from early to late in his career, must be noted.[43]

Thus many of Sartre's statements that appear to support the interpretation of human reality as pure freedom may well be more a matter of exaggeration than a different view of human reality.

My second reason for adopting the position that facticity is best understood as playing an integral role in human reality, as Sartre understood it, is that two of the concepts that appear in *Being and Nothingness*, namely embodiment and bad faith, become unintelligible unless the second interpretation is adopted. The concept of bad faith will receive extensive treatment in the next chapter, and I will leave an examination of it until then. For now we will turn to the concept of embodiment.

As we have seen, consciousness is the activity of a being. That being is a body and it is the body that provides much of being-for-itself's facticity. While the body can exist in the mode of an object in the world (an object that has a certain weight, length, history, race, sex, and so on), it is also by virtue of being-for-itself's embodiment that it can be conscious. It is the body that provides being-for-itself with a perspective, a place in the world, from which being-for-itself moves into the future.[44] But the body is not a mere instrument for being-for-itself. Sartre writes that "being-for-itself must be wholly body and it must be wholly consciousness; it can not be *united* with a body."[45] They cannot be "united" as this would imply initial separation. Rather the for-itself is bodily. The body is "in no way a contingent addition to my soul; on the contrary it is a permanent structure of my being and the permanent condition of possibility for my consciousness as consciousness *of* the world and as a transcendent project toward my future" (328). It is through its embodiment that being-for-itself has being-in-the-world, existing as a concretely situated freedom. Sartre presents the body as an integral part of being-for-itself, of human reality, even making being-for-itself a possibility, claiming: "In the same way that the body conditions consciousness as pure consciousness of the world, it renders consciousness possible even in its very freedom" (328). While the body does not determine consciousness, Sartre allows that it does condition it, and it does so through providing being-for-itself with its position in the world, a position that, though not reducing the freedom of being-for-itself to choose, does limit what can be chosen. The human subject as an embodied consciousness in the world will appear as a recurring theme in future chapters.

Having established some of the central concepts in Sartre's treatment of consciousness and ontology, and having settled on an interpretation of human reality as an ambiguous relation of transcendence and facticity, I will now move on to an examination of Sartre's account of what happens when one refuses to accept this human condition.

NOTES

1. Sartre, "Intentionality," 4.

2. It should be noted that while Sartre owed a great debt to Husserl, he was also highly critical of Husserl's "pure" phenomenology. A succinct account of criticisms leveled at Husserl by Sartre, and other existentialists, can be found in David E. Cooper, *Existentialism*, 39–56.

3. Sartre, *Being and Nothingness*, xxvii.

4. Sartre, "Consciousness of Self," 122.

5. Sartre, "Intentionality," 4.

6. Sartre, *Being and Nothingness*, xxvii.

7. I borrow these terms from Gregory McCulloch, *Using Sartre*, 87–88.

8. See, for example, René Descartes, *Meditations on First Philosophy*.

9. Joseph P. Fell's introduction to Sartre, "Intentionality," 4.

10. Sartre, "Intentionality," 4.

11. Sartre, *Being and Nothingness*, 8–9.

12. Elsewhere Sartre writes, "we are not able to conceive an infinite regress of consciousness, save as a joke" (Sartre, "Consciousness of Self," 122).

13. Sartre, *The Transcendence of the Ego*, 48–49.

14. Sartre, *Being and Nothingness*, 150.

15. Sartre, *The Transcendence of the Ego*, 53.

16. Sartre, *Being and Nothingness*, 151.

17. Sartre claims that "the *nothing* which separates" the two terms of reflection (the reflective and the reflected-on) "divides them more profoundly" than in the case of the for-itself. Sartre, *Being and Nothingness*, 152.

18. Sartre, *Being and Nothingness*, xliii. Sartre's distinction between the being of objects (being-in-itself) and conscious being (being-for-itself) should not be confused with Cartesian dualism, which holds that there are two kinds of substance, material and mental. For Sartre, in this context, *being* refers to a mode or manner of existing rather than an entity or substance. It will emerge that the same entity, "man," can participate in both modes of being.

19. Thomas W. Busch, *The Power of Consciousness*, 23. Busch provides a thorough account of being-in-itself in this work, 22–30.

20. Sartre, *Being and Nothingness*, xli–xlii.

21. The idea that one can objectify, and be objectified by, others plays a vital role in a Sartrean account of oppression and will receive extensive treatment in later chapters.

22. Hazel E. Barnes, "Sartre's Ontology," 15.

23. Sartre, *Being and Nothingness*, 617.

24. A good discussion on Sartre's references to freedom with respect to the reflective and pre-reflective modes of consciousness, which I have made use of here, can be found in Michael Hammond, Jane Howarth, and Russell Keat, *Understanding Phenomenology*, 116–24.

25. Sartre, *Being and Nothingness*, 31–32.

26. We might even ask ourselves "What difference would it make if in fact we were determined?" How, for example, would this knowledge change the way we approach a restaurant menu?

27. Sartre, *Being and Nothingness*, xli.

28. Elsewhere Sartre writes: "Man is, before all else, something which propels itself towards a future" (Sartre, *Existentialism and Humanism*, 28).

29. The passage "is what it is not and . . . is not what it is" can also be interpreted in terms of reflective consciousness: being-for-itself is (as reflective consciousness) what it is not (the object of reflection), and it is not (as reflective consciousness) what it is (the object of reflection).

30. Barnes, "Sartre's Ontology," 15.

31. Sartre, *Being and Nothingness*, 83.

32. Nonetheless, it is still profitable to make the distinction between transcendence and facticity for the purposes of discussing bad faith. This will become apparent in chapter 2 where two forms of bad faith, each turning on one or other of these aspects, is discussed.

33. Thomas C. Anderson offers an excellent account of these two interpretations of human reality in *Being and Nothingness* in his *Sartre's Two Ethics*, 14–26.

34. Sartre, *Being and Nothingness*, 440–41.

35. Maurice Merleau-Ponty, for example, accuses Sartre of being a "a good Cartesian," and of conducting a "philosophy of the pure subject." Merleau-Ponty, "Sartre and Ultrabolshevism," in his *Adventures of the Dialectic*, 147 and 98 respectively.

36. Sartre, *Being and Nothingness*, 484.

37. In calling Sartre's conception of freedom "negative," I am not aligning it with Isaiah Berlin's notion of "negative freedom," which appears in the essay "Two Concepts of Liberty," in his *Four Essays on Liberty*, 118–72. While both Sartre's and Berlin's negative freedoms stand in contrast to the "positive freedom" to achieve goals, Berlin's negative freedom is freedom from obstacles. Sartre's negative freedom (my term) is best understood as "not determined." As we have seen, Sartre holds that obstacles are essential to freedom.

38. Sartre, *Being and Nothingness*, 483.

39. David Detmer claims that there are two senses of *freedom* to be found in Sartre's early writings, which he (Detmer) terms *ontological freedom* and *practical freedom* (Detmer, *Freedom as a Value*, 57ff.). Ontological freedom is freedom in the sense of "not determined," while practical freedom is freedom in the sense of "freedom of obtaining." Interpreting freedom in this way, Detmer claims that we can allow that the slave is as free as the master in terms of ontological freedom, though not in terms of practical freedom. Anderson criticizes Detmer's interpretation on the grounds that Detmer has a "minimalistic notion of Sartre's ontological freedom" that is incompatible with "Sartre's assertions about human freedom being total, absolute, unlimited, wholly free, and so forth" and that these assertions "mean that freedom is not limited or conditioned *at all* by its facticity" (Anderson, *Sartre's Two Ethics*, 176–77).

40. Sartre, *Being and Nothingness*, 83.

41. Anderson, *Sartre's Two Ethics*, 24.

42. Sartre, *Being and Nothingness*, 550.

43. Linda Bell, *Sartre's Ethics of Authenticity*, 31. As to why Sartre is so often "prone to overstatement" when writing of freedom, I suspect that it may be due in part to the intellectual climate in which he was writing. With Marxism and psychoanalysis (both of which could be interpreted as deterministic theories) as perhaps the dominant schools of thought at the time, any claims to individual freedom would have run very much against the

current of contemporary thought. As such, this perhaps helped forge a defensive evangelism resulting in exaggerated (and unwise) claims. Further research on this point would be needed to make it stand.

44. An account of Sartre's approach to embodiment can be found in Xavier O. Monasterio, "The Body in *Being and Nothingness*," 50–62.

45. Sartre, *Being and Nothingness*, 305.

2

Bad Faith, Human Being, and Self-Deception

In types of oppression, such as racism and sexism, it may be the case that the oppressor is observed to treat or apprehend the other as being somewhat less than the complex being that Sartre claims we all are. Most typically, in such cases, the oppressor ignores the freedom and subjectivity of the other, by treating the other as some kind of object; for example, a racially determined (and inferior) being in the case of racism, a sex object or tool in the case of sexism. The oppressor attenuates the being of the other such that the other can be incorporated into the oppressor's simplified world. However, what is of particular interest to us in the context of this book is that the oppressor can be seen to attenuate not only the being of the other, but his or her own being as well. This attenuation of being, which fails to recognize or accommodate the ambiguity of human reality, is *bad faith*.

The ambiguity of the human condition, whereby one participates in both being-for-itself and being-in-itself, is something that one may desire to disrupt, often as a way of reacting to a difficult social situation or the presence of an other. Sartre believes that while these two basic modes of being can be validly coordinated, often they are not.[1] Instead, a person may, through self-deception, attempt to deny one or other of their modes of being. Sartre labels attempts such as these *bad faith*. The "badness" of bad faith lies in its inauthenticity. Authenticity requires a recognition and coordination of the two aspects of human being, as it is only through this that situated freedom can be appreciated and nurtured. Bad faith, in its attempt to disrupt human reality, cannot result in authentic human being. By denying, ignoring, or playing down either one's transcendence or facticity, one avoids facing one's true status as a freedom in situation.

The concept of bad faith, however, is a complex one and, as it plays a crucial role in a Sartrean account of oppression, it is worthy of detailed analysis. The aim of this chapter is twofold. First, it will examine some of Sartre's examples of ways of dealing with being human that involve bad faith. A point that I will stress, and one that is too infrequently raised in the literature, is that bad faith admits of two types: one involving a denial of transcendence, the other a denial of facticity. The second aim of the chapter will be to provide an account of how self-deception is caught up in the operation of bad faith.

BAD FAITH AND HUMAN BEING

Examples and Styles of Bad Faith

Let us begin by examining some of the examples of bad faith that appear in *Being and Nothingness*. The first example is of a woman in a café on a first date with a particular man. The man puts the woman in a difficult situation in which she finds herself pressured to abandon her ambiguity and make a choice between objectivity and subjectivity.

According to Sartre, the woman knows full well that the man harbors sexual desire for her and is hoping to seduce her. She also knows that sooner or later she will have to decide whether to accept or reject his advances:

> She is profoundly aware of the desire which she inspires, but the desire cruel and naked would humiliate and horrify her. Yet she would find no charm in a respect which would be only respect. In order to satisfy her, there must be a feeling which is addressed wholly to her *personality*— i.e., to her full freedom—and which would be a recognition of her freedom. But at the same time this feeling must be wholly desire; that is, it must address itself to her body as object. (55)[2]

While she is unwilling to decide to go along with his plans for the two of them, she does enjoy the attention he gives her. Her solution to her predicament is to disarm his behavior of its sexual connotations, refusing to apprehend it as conduct aimed at making "the first approach" (55). She does this by stripping his behavior of its character as part of a temporal development toward an end, that is to say, its character as a project, instead bestowing upon it immediate meanings. So, for example, if he says "I find you so attractive," she interprets this as referring to the immediate present, such that the phrase is an appraisal of her as a conversationalist (they are, after all, now in the midst of conversation) rather than as a precursor or invitation to physical intimacy. She interprets his behavior and utterances simply as they stand.

> The man who is speaking to her appears to her sincere and respectful as the table is round or square, as the wall coloring is blue or gray. The qualities thus attached to the person she is listening to are in this way fixed in a permanence like that of things, which is no other than the projection of the strict present of the qualities into the temporal flux. (55)

So far, the woman has succeeded in avoiding the decision to accept or refuse the man's advances by interpreting them as being something else. But suppose the man were to take her hand. Sartre assumes that such an act could not fail to be interpreted as an expression of sexual desire, thus putting more pressure on the woman to decide either way. Sartre claims that for her to leave her hand there would be to consent to the man's advances, while withdrawing it would be a rejection that would "break the troubled and unstable harmony which gives the hour its charm" (55). However, the woman wants to further postpone the decision. How can she do this, given the situation?

> We know what happens next; the young woman leaves her hand there, but she *does not notice* that she is leaving it. She does not notice because it happens by chance that she is at this moment all intellect. She draws her companion up to the most lofty regions of sentimental speculation; she speaks of Life, of her life, she shows herself in her essential aspect—a personality, a consciousness. And during this time the divorce of the body from the soul is accomplished; the hand rests inert between the warm hands of her companion—neither consenting nor resisting—a thing. (55–56)

Sartre claims that this woman is in bad faith. He identifies several procedures that she uses to achieve this state. First, she reduces the actions of her companion to the in-itself by refusing to interpret them as components of a project and instead taking them simply at face value as being just what they are in isolation from a project. Second, she interprets his behavior as not being what it is, by taking his flattery to be directed at her purely as a free subject. Finally she, in a sense, disembodies herself, that is, "realizes herself as *not being* her own body, and she contemplates it as though from above as a passive object to which events can *happen* but which can neither provoke them nor avoid them" (56). What do these moves have in common? Sartre's answer is that they all involve the use of facticity and transcendence, that double property of human being. He explains:

> These two aspects of human reality are and ought to be capable of a valid coordination. But bad faith does not wish either to coordinate them nor surmount them in a synthesis. Bad faith seeks to affirm their identity while preserving their differences. It must affirm facticity as *being* transcendence and transcendence as *being* facticity, in such a way that at the instant when a person apprehends the one, he can find himself abruptly faced with the other. (56)

Sartre is claiming here that when, for example, the woman interprets the man's utterance "I find you so attractive" as referring simply to the immediate situation of the conversation, she is reducing the utterance to its facticity (that it is made here and now in the midst of conversation, that it consists of the words "I find you so attractive," and so on) while ignoring the project that transcends the utterance. In other words, she takes the utterance, which can be interpreted from the perspectives of facticity *and* transcendence, and interprets it purely as facticity. Similarly, she reduces her companion to the in-itself, attributing his apparent qualities (for example, his apparent respect and sincerity) to him in a way parallel to the attribution of qualities such as shape and color to objects. By objectifying him in this way, she is able to ignore his existence as a subject engaged in a project and whose behavior and utterances form part of that project.

Thus the woman's bad faith consists in reducing something (the man or his behavior) that consists of both facticity and transcendence to facticity only. But this is only half of the story, for while she reduces her companion to facticity alone, she reduces herself to transcendence alone. She ignores her presence in the world of objects through divorcing herself from her body. Her body becomes a mere object to which things can happen. While it is true that the body is an object to which things can happen, it is not simply that. The body is also the subject in the world. More particularly, the woman's body is her being-in-the-world as a subject *and* her being-in-the-midst-of-the-world as an object. By divorcing herself from her body when her companion takes her hand, she becomes "all intellect" and contemplates her body "as though from above." She attenuates her being, taking herself to be simply transcendence.

Sartre claims that bad faith involves the utilization of the double property of facticity and transcendence. But facticity/transcendence is not the only pair of concepts that he uses to describe the ambiguity of human being. There are also *being-in-the-midst-of-the-world/being-in-the-world* and *being-for-others/being-for-itself*. The first terms of each pair (that is, facticity, being-in-the-midst-of-the-world, and being-for-others), while not identical, are similar in their being species of being-in-itself, partaking of an object-like being that conforms to the principle of identity. My facticity includes such things as my past acts, the limitations of my body, my situation, and so on. Although I, as a free being, can interpret these facts in various ways (as indeed I can with other objects), they are facts, with an existence in the world like objects. My being-in-the-midst-of-the-world is my presence in the world as other things are present in the world. While I am an agent, I am also a part of the landscape, a face in the crowd, or a body sitting on a bench under a tree in the garden. My being-for-others (which we will examine in more detail in chapter 4) is my being as a part of the world of another. It is a judgment that I infer from the gaze of another, and that I experience as an objective component of my situation.

On the other hand, the second terms of each of the pairs (namely, transcendence, being-in-the-world, and being-for-itself), while again, not identical, are similar in their connection with being-for-itself. In transcendence I, through negation, separate myself as a free, future-directed being, from my facticity and the objects in my world. My being-in-the-world (as opposed to my being-in-the-midst-of-the-world where I exist as a part of the world on a plane with other such parts) is my being as a free and active agent in a world interpreted in the light of my projects. Finally, my being-for-itself, when taken as part of the pair being-for-others/being-for-itself, is my being-for-myself (my experience of myself as a free, undetermined being), as opposed to my being-for-others, in which I exist as an object for an other.

The ambiguity of human being is such that one participates in both of the modes of being in each of the pairs of concepts. One is both facticity *and* transcendence, both being-in-the-midst-of-the-world *and* being-in-the-world, both being-for-others *and* being-for-itself. In bad faith, however, the attempt is made to resolve the ambiguity of human being by the attenuation or simplification of being through a total identification with one mode of being and/or the denial of the other. As we have seen, Sartre's example of the woman in the café stands as an illustration of this. For example, her response to the man taking her hand involves the utilization of two of the double properties of human being, namely being-in-the-midst-of-the-world/being-in-the-world and facticity/transcendence. First, she attenuates the being of her hand. Her hand has both being-in-the-midst-of-the-world, as an object in the world, and being-in-the-world, as a part of her embodied subjectivity, but she interprets it as partaking purely of the former, seeing it as a thing, an object. And, of course, she is partly right. Her hand *is* an object in the world (having being-in-the-midst-of-the-world), but it is not only that. It is also a part of her as an embodied subject (being-in-the-world), an actor and not simply something acted upon. Second, she attenuates her being as a whole by divorcing herself from the hand. She dissociates herself from this hand, which is a part of her facticity, in favor of transcendence. Again, she is partly right. She *does* partake of transcendence, but not *only* that. She also has facticity and is a bodily presence in the world. The hand is a part of her and, given the situation she is in, a particularly significant part of her, as it is, in a sense, her hand or its activity that may well determine the outcome of the evening.

Before moving on with our examination of examples of bad faith, we should pause to consider a criticism that has been leveled at the example we have just discussed. While the case of the woman in the café does provide an illustration of attempted ontological manipulations that are examples of bad faith, there are aspects of Sartre's example that are highly problematic. In particular, Sartre appears to be harsh in his judgment that the woman is in bad faith, primarily at least, in refusing "to apprehend the [man's] desire for what it is" (55). Toril Moi argues that any plausibility of the description in the mind of the reader rests on the reader's knowledge of the man's motives.[3] *We* know that the man harbors sexual desire for the woman and we know that his behavior should be interpreted as aimed at "the first approach," but we do so because Sartre tells us that from the start. What of the woman? Should we expect *her* to interpret the man's behavior in this way? Sartre does, and Moi is highly critical of this.

Moi argues that flirtation (Sartre refers to what is going on in his example as flirting)[4] "is based on ambiguity: it is a game in which one does not declare one's hand."[5] To assume that the woman "knows" what is "really" going on is to assume too much. The ambiguity of flirting makes misrecognition of its aims a live possibility. We cannot assume that the woman will, or indeed should, interpret the man's behavior as Sartre does.

Moi's criticism seems justified, and it reveals a tension that can be found in much of Sartre's work. Sartre's ontology and account of human being is one in which one often meets with complexity and ambiguity. Yet at times, and the case of the woman in the café is a good example of this, he overlooks his own insights on this matter, presenting situations as quite clear and unambiguous. To Sartre it is just obvious that the behavior of the man in the café has the aim that Sartre attributes to it, even though it does not explicitly state its aim and, if anything, disguises it. The example also reveals that while Sartre is concerned with the situatedness of freedom, he at times displays ignorance and insensitivity to the situation of those of whom he speaks. He assumes, for example, that the woman should interpret the man's behavior as the man does. Is it right to assume that a woman (or indeed anyone in a situation other than the man in question) will have the same access to, and the same freedom with respect to, the same meanings of behavior given by Sartre and the man? Moi thinks not (125–33), and I agree with her. Further to this, Sartre's insensitivity to the woman's situation inadvertently reveals the role the wider social situation (in this case the significance of sexual difference with respect to desire) plays in limiting freedom. It points to both the ambiguity of the woman's situation and the difficulties that this ambiguity can pose.

We have seen in the example of the woman in the café the use of the double concepts of facticity/transcendence and being-in-the-midst-of-the-world/being-in-the-world in bad faith. Sartre gives a further example of bad faith that utilizes the double concept of being-for-others/being-for-itself. This is the example of a waiter who, Sartre claims, behaves a bit too much like a waiter.

> His movement is quick and forward, a little too precise, a little too rapid. He comes toward the patrons with a step a little too quick. He bends forward a little too eagerly; his voice, his eyes express an interest a little too solicitous for the order of the customer. Finally there he returns, trying to imitate in his walk the inflexible stiffness of some kind of automaton while carrying his tray with the recklessness of a tight-rope-walker by putting it in a perpetually unstable, perpetually broken equilibrium which he perpetually reestablishes by a light movement of the hand and arm.[6]

The waiter, Sartre claims, "is playing at *being* a waiter" (59). The waiter understands that the customers of the café have an idea of how a waiter behaves. There is an image, from the perspective of an observer, of what a waiter is like. This is the waiter's being-for-others, and the waiter's behavior betrays an attempt to realize the condition of being a waiter as seen from the outside, to become his being-for-others. Sartre points out that there can often be social pressure put upon people, such as waiters, to instantiate the public image that accompanies their profession:

> This obligation is not different from that which is imposed on all tradesmen. Their condition is wholly one of ceremony. The public demands of them that they realize it as a ceremony; there is the dance of the grocer, an auctioneer, a tailor. A grocer who dreams is offensive to the buyer, because such a grocer is not wholly a grocer. (59)

In identifying himself with his being-for-others, the waiter is in bad faith, denying his being-for-itself by becoming a waiter-automaton, a thing that is totally predictable and incapable of acting otherwise.

The waiter's bad faith can also be interpreted in terms of facticity/transcendence. Sartre claims that the waiter tries to *be* a waiter "in the sense that this inkwell is an inkwell, or the glass *is* a glass" (59). That is, he tries to identify himself solely with his facticity, his profession in particular. Of course, he *is* a waiter, in the sense that he *is not* a fireman or a dentist. But if he is one, he is not so in the mode of being-in-itself that he seems to be attempting to realize. Being a waiter means all sorts of things: leaving home at a certain time, setting up the restaurant, brewing the coffee, and so on. The waiter may take these duties as things he automatically fulfils in his waiter objectness, "but all these concepts, all these judgments refer to the transcendent" (60). Although these aspects are a part of the job that is the waiter's facticity, the waiter is more than his facticity, as evidenced by the reference these duties make to a subject engaged in a project. The difficulty of the waiter's situation, which ends in bad faith, is, as we have just seen, that there can be social demands on one such as a waiter to realize their occupation and *be* just that. The temptation to turn to bad faith may be great. Nonetheless living in bad faith must still be seen as a choice, although, given some social situations, it is a difficult choice to avoid.

Apart from the double concepts of facticity/transcendence, being-in-the-midst-of-the-world/being-in-the-world, and being-for-others/being-for-itself, bad faith can also make use of what Sartre calls *temporal ekstases*. Here Sartre is referring to a further ambiguity in human being concerning one's past acts, more specifically the ambiguity of being both what one has been and not being what one has been. It will be recalled from the discussion of freedom in chapter 1 that in reflecting on the past, being-for-itself recognizes itself as both being that which is reflected on and, as the reflector, not being that which is reflected on. The object of the reflection (in this case, the past self) is an aspect of the facticity of the self that the self-reflecting transcends. Thus there are parallels between the temporal ekstases and the pair facticity/transcendence.

My past acts are a part of my facticity, and to the extent that I am my facticity I am my past acts. But I am not only that. I am not simply a determined object, I am a free and transcendent being and so I am also not my past acts. In bad faith, however, one can attempt to resolve this ambiguity by identifying wholly with one of these relations to one's past. Thus there can be

the man who deliberately *arrests himself* at one period in his life and refuses to take into consideration the later changes . . . [or] the man who in the face of reproaches or rancor dissociates himself from his past by insisting on his freedom and on his perpetual recreation. (58)

The example Sartre gives to illustrate this type of bad faith is of a man with a history of engaging in homosexual activity and who "while recognizing his homosexual inclination, while avowing each and every particular misdeed which he has committed, refuses with all his strength to consider himself '*a paederast*'" (63).[7]

The man recognizes his past actions, but wishes to distance himself from them, lest they constitute his destiny.

> He does not wish to let himself be considered as a thing. He has an ob-
> scure but strong feeling that an homosexual is not an homosexual as
> this table is a table or as this red-haired man is red-haired. It seems to
> him that he has escaped from each mistake as soon as he has posited it
> and recognized it; he even feels that the psychic duration by itself
> cleanses him from each misdeed, constitutes for him an undetermined
> future, causes him to be born anew. (64)

Sartre acknowledges that the man is trading on a very significant truth of human being as being-for-itself. He is right in not allowing his be-ing to be subsumed under the category of being a homosexual in the mode of being-in-itself. However, at the same time, he misuses this truth, utilizing it as a mode of escaping "the terrible judgment of col-lectivity" and a past he would rather disown, rather than as the basis for future self-creation. He does this by playing on the word *being*. Sartre writes:

> He would be right actually if he understood the phrase, "I am not a
> paederast" in the sense of "I am not what I am." That is, if he declared
> to himself, "To the extent that a pattern of conduct is defined as the con-
> duct of a paederast and to the extent that I have adopted this conduct,
> I am a paederast. But to the extent that human reality can not be finally
> defined by patterns of conduct I am not one." But instead he slides sur-
> reptitiously towards a different connotation of the word "being." He un-
> derstands "not being" in the sense of "not-being-in-itself." He lays claim
> to "not being a paederast" in the sense in which this table *is not* an
> inkwell. He is in bad faith. (64)

In other words, the man is in bad faith by virtue of his having attenu-ated the word *being*, taking it to refer simply to the being of objects. The man is correct in not accepting an evaluation of himself as *being* a homosexual in the way that a car *is* red. However, by taking *being* to refer only to the mode of being-in-itself, he allows himself to take the illegitimate step of ignoring the fact that he has, at least up until now, been engaged in a project that has included homosexual activity. Of course, as a free being, the man may choose never again to engage in such a project. That way can never be barred. However, to the extent that he is still engaged in this project he is a homosexual, in the sense that the waiter can legitimately claim to *be* a waiter (not in the mode of being an object, but rather in the sense that he is not a diplomat). Similarly, if he has renounced this project, he is still required by Sartre to accept that he *was* or *has been* a homosexual in this relevant sense. To avoid bad faith the man must accept that he is, in a relevant sense, a homosexual, while accepting also that he has choice with respect to his sexual conduct.

This is an interesting case that highlights the importance of understanding that Sartre allows for two types of bad faith. The man denies his attachment to his past, thereby attempting to distance himself from his facticity and live a pure transcendence. Now, in terms of simplistic interpretations of Sartre's account of human being, which portray it as allowing or requiring one to utterly renounce or disconnect oneself from one's past and one's facticity in general, the man would stand as an example of an authentic person living the ideal of Sartrean freedom. Yet Sartre is clear in labeling the man's denial of facticity as an example of bad faith, thereby adding support to the thesis that human reality is best understood as situated freedom wherein facticity must be seen to play an important role.

Bad faith is made possible by the fact that "human reality, in its most immediate being, in the intrastructure of the pre-reflective cogito, must be what it is not and not be what it is" (67). In fact, the role that Sartre gives the phenomenon of bad faith in the thesis of *Being and Nothingness* is of great importance because it is through an analysis of bad faith that Sartre argues that human reality has this nature; that is, being what it is not and not being what it is. The maneuvers that constitute bad faith require that human reality be like this. It is only through pre-reflective recognition that I am not wholly my facticity, and thus *not* (in any simple sense) my facticity, that I can affirm totally my transcendence, as the homosexual does. But it is to the extent that I am my facticity that I am able to affirm it as the totality of my being, as we saw the waiter do. The same goes, mutatis mutandis, for transcendence.

It is also through recognition of the reality of human being that we can see that bad faith can never succeed fully in its aims. Bad faith is an escape, but it is an unstable one. To the extent that I evaluate myself as being in the mode of the in-itself, I must work hard to ignore that I as the one evaluating must, in the process of evaluating, exist in the mode of the for-itself. Conversely, to the extent that I confine my being to transcendence, I must continually ignore the gaze of others and the traces of me that I leave in the material world that must confront me at every turn with my facticity. The role played by motivated ignorance in bad faith will be examined later in this chapter.

Two Interpretations of Bad Faith

I have stressed that bad faith can entail a flight toward facticity and a denial of transcendence, or a flight toward transcendence and a denial of facticity. It is important to note, however, that several commentators and critics have not interpreted bad faith in this way. Rather, they say, bad faith consists only in a denial of transcendence.[8] For example, in an early commentary on Sartre's philosophy, Mary Warnock claims: "Bad Faith consists in pretending to ourselves and to others that things could not be otherwise—that we are bound to our way of life, and that we could not escape it even if we wanted to."[9] More contemporary examples of commentators who present bad faith as simply involving a flight toward facticity include Michèle Le Doeuff and Toril Moi. Le Doeuff claims that "bad faith consists in the refusal to recognize oneself as a free subject and the pretence of being determined,"[10] and that when "the for-itself is degraded into an in-itself and freedom into facticity, in short there is bad faith."[11] Moi writes: "To pretend to have no choice is to deny freedom, and that, precisely, is *the very definition* of bad faith."[12] As we have seen, while it is true that Sartre thinks that people do the sort of thing that these authors have described, and that when they do they are in bad faith, this is not the only configuration that bad faith can have. Bad faith can also consist in a denial of facticity or a total identification with transcendence.

It would be legitimate to claim that bad faith is simply a denial of freedom if *freedom* is taken to refer to *situated freedom*. Situated freedom, in which one is free within the limits of a situation, contains the elements of both transcendence and facticity and is thereby compatible with the portrait of the human condition discussed in chapter 1. Thus, in claiming that bad faith consists in the denial of situated freedom, the two types of bad faith are accommodated, as both flights from transcendence and flights from facticity would constitute denials of situated freedom. However, the passages quoted above are open to being interpreted as employing the more restricted sense of freedom as pure transcendence, leading to an interpretation of bad faith that characterizes it as a denial of transcendence only. This interpretation limits bad faith to one form and fails to recognize the ambiguous human condition and the situated freedom from which bad faith is an attempt to escape.

I suspect that this interpretation springs from two sources. First, it is undoubtedly the case that in *Being and Nothingness* Sartre puts more emphasis on describing the free, transcendent aspect of human being and, given this, perhaps the cases of bad faith involving a denial of this transcendence appear more striking or important. Second, the first mention of bad faith in *Being and Nothingness*, which occurs in the chapter entitled "The Origin of Negation," does suggest that bad faith is a flight from transcendence. However, this occurs in the context of a discussion on anguish (the awareness one has of one's transcendence) and so, in introducing the notion of bad faith in such a context, it is natural that it should stress bad faith as an escape from transcendence. But in the chapter following, entitled "Bad Faith," there can be little doubt that Sartre intends bad faith to be understood as an attempt to escape the ambiguity of a human being's partaking of transcendence *and facticity*, and thus allows bad faith to take either of two general forms (an escape from transcendence or an escape from facticity). He does not intend bad faith to be simply interpreted as a flight from transcendence.

As we have seen, the example of the homosexual clearly entails a flight from facticity, which Sartre explicitly refers to as bad faith. It is interesting to note that Warnock, in presenting bad faith as referring merely to a flight toward facticity, only discusses Sartre's examples of bad faith that take that form. She cites only the example of the waiter, which involves identification with being-for-others, and the example of the woman in the café.[13] With regard to the latter, Warnock follows

the course of Sartre's story up to the point where the woman objectifies her hand (an instance that Warnock legitimately identifies as a
flight toward facticity), but stops short of the point where the woman
distances herself from her body and her situation (a clear example of
a flight toward transcendence, rather than toward facticity).

However, having said this, I must acknowledge that there *is* a sense
in which all cases of bad faith involve the adoption of a static, complete mode of being. Lewis Gordon describes this aspect of bad faith
as follows:

> [Bad faith] involves taking refuge in a form of being what I "really am,"
> as though my "real" being is as static and as complete as a stone. I can
> try to take refuge away from myself as a conscious being and take ad-
> vantage of my situation of also being presented to others as a being sub-
> ject to their interpretation of me. I can claim that other people have
> knowledge of a self that *is* "me" but that that self is not really me. Or I
> may claim that the self that is presented to others is the real me. In ei-
> ther case, it is another effort to take refuge in what I "really am."[14]

Here Gordon is describing bad faith particularly as it relates to the
double property of being-for-others/being-for-itself. The flight toward
being-for-others (the latter of the two examples in the quoted passage) as a flight toward facticity can easily be thought of in terms of
the pursuit of a static and complete identity; after all, we are here in
the realm of the in-itself, the mode of being of objects that, by definition, complies with the principle of identity. Yet the former example,
in which one disowns one's being-for-others, is less easy to understand in terms of being static and complete. How can I, as Sartre puts
it, "affirm . . . that I *am* my transcendence in the mode of being of a
thing"?[15] Is it not the case that transcendence is the antithesis of being
"a thing"? I interpret the point to be that while transcendence itself
cannot be a thing, one can affirm in bad faith that one *is* one's transcendence in a style similar to the claim that a table *is* round. Thus the
positing of an *identity* between the self and transcendence, in the
same way as we understand objects to be identical with themselves,
is a matter of bad faith. As Gordon puts it in the quoted passage
above, transcendence becomes what I "really am" in a manner parallel to the other form of bad faith where I affirm my facticity as being

what "I really am." Treating transcendence or freedom as a fixed quality, like color or shape in objects, is to miss the point of transcendence or freedom as the process by which one makes oneself.

It does seem clear, however, that there are indeed two general types of bad faith: one in which the for-itself denies its transcendence, the other in which the for-itself denies its facticity. Chapters 3 and 5 will each examine an oppressive scenario involving bad faith. The bad faith present in chapter 3's example will be shown to be of the first type (bad faith as a denial of transcendence) while the case discussed in chapter 5 will be shown to involve the second type of bad faith (bad faith as a denial of facticity). In each of these cases the type of bad faith at play is significant in understanding the motives and behavior of the oppressor.

Before moving on to the next chapter, there is an aspect of bad faith that requires investigation: namely, how it is that bad faith can occur, given Sartre's theory of consciousness. Thus far, we have seen the relationship between bad faith and human being, bad faith's nature as an attenuation of human being aimed at a resolution (or dissolution) of the ambiguity of human being. In the next section, we shall examine bad faith's character as a species of self-deception. Some commentators have suggested that, given Sartre's account of consciousness as translucent, he is unable to accommodate the possibility of self-deception, thus rendering bad faith incoherent in the context of his model of consciousness. We must seek to understand how, given Sartre's model of consciousness, such self-deception is possible.

BAD FAITH AND SELF-DECEPTION

To this point we have examined bad faith in terms of its (attempted) ontological consequences, namely the denial of human reality. However, Sartre claims that the ontological maneuvers that characterize bad faith are conducted on the level of belief, and so there are epistemic issues to be considered as well (67–70). The waiter believes that he is a waiter-automaton; the homosexual man believes that his past has no effect on him. The denial of transcendence or facticity occurs on the level of belief, yet for Sartre *belief* need not be understood as referring only to a reflectively held mental item. For example, Sartre judges that the waiter is in bad faith and (implicitly) that the waiter believes he is a waiter-automaton, on the basis of the waiter's behavior. The waiter behaves in a manner that suggests that he has particular beliefs about himself and, in virtue of this, Sartre attributes those beliefs to him, regardless of whether the waiter has ever actually articulated these beliefs to himself.[16] Ambiguous human reality is an ever-present fact about us, so bad faith beliefs that deny this human reality are false. Yet, Sartre is clear, bad faith beliefs are not the result of unfortunate deficits in knowledge, nor are they the results of innocent errors in reasoning. Rather, bad faith beliefs result from self-deception. That bad faith is a matter of self-deception is an important point to raise in the context of the current work, which argues that we can understand some aspects of oppression as involving bad faith. It is by revealing that bad faith beliefs about the self and others (beliefs that can play a role in oppression) are a matter of self-deception, rather than innocent error, that we can see the oppressor's beliefs as motivated and actively adopted, beliefs for which we may hold her responsible.

Bad faith, Sartre tells us, is a matter of self-deception. He writes:

> Bad faith . . . is indeed a lie to oneself. To be sure, the one who practices bad faith is hiding a displeasing truth or presenting as truth a pleasing untruth. Bad faith then has in appearance a structure of falsehood. Only what changes everything is the fact that in bad faith it is from myself that I am hiding the truth. Thus the duality of the deceiver and the deceived does not exist here. Bad faith on the contrary implies in essence the unity of a *single* consciousness.[17]

The idea that self-deception can occur within "the unity of a single consciousness" is not an easy one to understand. A reason for this is that, on the surface at least, the concept of self-deception would appear to harbor a paradox. Alfred Mele calls this paradox "the paradox of belief" and formulates it as follows:

> For any A and B, when A deceives B into believing that p, A knows or truly believes that not-p while causing B to believe that p. So when A deceives A (i.e., himself) into believing that p, he knows or truly believes that not-p while causing himself to believe that p. Thus, A must simultaneously believe that not-p and believe that p. But how is this possible?[18]

In a case of one person deceiving another, the deceiver leads the other to believe something that the deceiver herself does not believe. But in self-deception the roles of deceiver and deceived appear to be played by the same person. In other words, it would seem that a self-deceived person must, at some point at least, believe both p and not-p, and this would seem to be a contradiction. If bad faith is a matter of self-deception, and if bad faith actually occurs (which Sartre clearly thinks it does), then it must be possible to give an account of bad faith that overcomes the paradox of belief that haunts notions of self-deception. How, then, is bad faith/self-deception possible?[19]

Bad Faith and Belief

One of the keys to Sartre's explanation of the possibility of self-deception is his particular account of what it is to believe something. He writes:

> The true problem of bad faith stems evidently from the fact that bad faith is *faith*. It can not be either a cynical lie or certainty—if certainty is the intuitive possession of the object. But if we take belief as meaning the adherence of being to its object when the object is not given or is given indistinctly, then bad faith is belief; and the essential problem of bad faith is a problem of belief.[20]

The "problem of belief" for Sartre is that, typically, belief involves disbelief. He explains: "To believe is to know that one believes, and to know that one believes is no longer to believe. Thus to believe is not to believe any longer because that is only to believe—this in the unity of one and the same non-thetic self-consciousness" (69). As has already been stated, a problem with the notion of self-deception is that it appears to be a contradiction for someone to both believe and disbelieve p. This trades on the assumption that belief in p entails not disbelieving p. However, if Sartre's formulation of belief is correct, and if belief is typically combined with disbelief, this assumption should be dropped. The statement "S believes p" does entail that it is not the case that S does not believe p. It would be contradictory to say that S believes p and it is false that S believes p. But given Sartre's account of belief, S's disbelief in p does not entail that it is false that S believes *p.* Rather, it entails that *S* both believes and disbelieves *p*, and it is not contradictory for *S* to both believe and disbelieve *p*.[21]

For Sartre, a belief is (at least often) not something that one either fully holds or fully rejects. A reason for this is that the evidence for or against a belief is often ambiguous or insufficient. While some of our beliefs will be supported by such a weight of evidence that they are virtually (if not in fact) indubitable, many or most of our beliefs are not like that. There can be greater and lesser degrees of evidence in support of a belief. An *ideal belief* would be one for which the evidence or justification were such that the belief would never require reevaluation. *Mere beliefs* (my term for beliefs that are combined with disbelief) are not of this character. They are based on insufficient evidence and fall short of what Allen Wood calls "the function of belief." Wood writes:

> We may look at all believing (including believing*) as a way of dealing with the world, and more especially with facts about this world as they present themselves to us in the form of direct sense information, reports heard or read, pieces of reasoning presented to or engaged in by our minds—in short, what we call, in relation to our beliefs, the "evidence" for them. Every belief is an attempt to "integrate" that evidence into a coherent whole. A belief of course tries to be consistent with all the evidence, but it also tries to explain this evidence, and it tries to do so in a tidy and nonarbitrary way. Finally, it tries to win out in a competition, using the above criteria as its standards, with other possibilities for belief which we see as alternatives to it.[22]

While not all (perhaps very few, if indeed any) beliefs would be ideal, in the sense of never requiring revision, they may still fulfill the function of belief, when interpreted as part of a process aimed at integrating the facts of the world. In the case of mere beliefs, the supporting evidence is deficient or ambiguous, and the mere belief does a poor job of integrating the facts of the world to which we have access.

Sartre claims that there are two attitudes that could be taken toward a mere belief: good faith and bad faith. "Good faith wishes to flee the 'not-believing-what-one-believes' by finding refuge in being."[23] This is to say that good faith wishes to overcome the imperfection of mere belief, to transform mere belief into some stronger belief. Good faith wants to be in a position to fully believe what it currently merely believes. It involves a critical attitude, seeking further evidence for a mere belief and being prepared to overturn a mere belief in the face of contrary evidence. What may start off as a mere belief, a matter of arbitrary faith, may be transformed into belief, something striving to fulfill the function of belief outlined above, when approached with the critical attitude of good faith.

Bad faith, however, "flees being by taking refuge in 'not-believing-what-it-believes'" (70). Bad faith realizes that mere belief is imperfect, but instead of trying to shore it up, it uses its imperfection to allow it to hold whatever it likes.

> Every belief is a belief that falls short; one never wholly believes what one believes. Consequently the primitive project of bad faith is only the utilization of this self-destruction of the fact of consciousness. If every belief in good faith is an impossible belief, then there is a place for every impossible belief. (69)

In bad faith the goal of good faith is taken to be the search for ideal beliefs (a goal that may be impossible to realize) and bad faith is made possible by this implicit belief. Joseph Catalano refers to this as bad faith's "bad-faith view of good faith."[24] Bad faith holds that a good faith approach to belief involves the quixotic goal of attaining ideal belief. Sartre writes:

> Consequently a peculiar type of evidence appears; *non-persuasive* evidence. Bad faith apprehends evidence but is resigned in advance to not being fulfilled by this evidence, to not being persuaded and transformed into good faith. It makes itself humble and modest; it is not ignorant, it says, that faith is decision and that after each intuition, it must decide and *will what it is.* Thus bad faith in its primitive project and in its coming into the world decides on the exact nature of its requirements. It stands forth in the firm resolution *not to demand too much,* to count itself satisfied when it is barely persuaded, to force itself in decisions to adhere to uncertain truths.[25]

Because no belief is perfectly justified, any belief is as good as any other: this is the rationale employed by bad faith.

While the function of beliefs may be the integration of evidence, that is not all that we relate our beliefs to. We also call on our beliefs in relation to our hopes and desires. It is from the desire to resolve the ambiguity of the human condition that people engage in bad faith. The man put the woman in the café in an uncomfortable position, a position she wished to avoid. The waiter did not want to confront his freedom. The homosexual did not want to confront his facticity. In each of these cases belief is used, not as a way of integrating evidence, but in the service of desire or the fleeing of uncomfortable truths. In bad faith, evidence is not the motivating force in the adoption of belief; fears and desires are.[26] Certainly, beliefs held in bad faith may rest on some evidence. In each of the cases of bad faith discussed so far, where one flees toward one's facticity (or transcendence), there is some truth to the matter. One *is*, to a degree, one's facticity (or transcendence), though one is not only that. In bad faith one attenuates one's being (or the being of another) by taking a belief, which may have some evidence in its favor, as being the whole story and requiring no further investigation.

In bad faith, one holds a belief for reasons other than epistemic ones, and one tries to be satisfied with that belief. However, in order to maintain the belief, one must be able to deal in some way with evidence that conflicts with it. Bad faith involves the obfuscation of such conflicting evidence, either by taking it as not actually being conflicting evidence (that is, as being, rather, evidence in support of the belief or at least not evidence that conflicts with the belief) or by avoiding focusing awareness on it altogether. Let us take the example of Sartre's waiter, who believes that he *is* a waiter in a fashion similar to that in which a table *is* a table. Recall that the waiter, in his role as a waiter, performs a variety of tasks that refer to abstract possibilities and projects that in turn refer to his freedom and transcendence. In order to maintain the belief that he is a waiter in the mode of being-in-itself, he must be able to avoid the realization that so much of his activity rests on his freedom, his being-for-itself. The waiter engages in activities that in part, at least, *constitute* his role, yet he acts as if his role is wholly given. He is somehow able to avoid realizing that his constituting activities entail certain attributes of himself that stand in contradiction to the attributes of a waiter-object.

So, the waiter does not take into account evidence that counts against his belief, enabling him to hold the belief. But this "not taking evidence into account" could be a matter of simply being mistaken. Perhaps he quite innocently overlooks it. If he is to be self-deceived, rather than simply mistaken, the avoidance of evidence must be more active than this: it must be motivated. And it is clear that Sartre takes bad faith to be motivated. But what mechanism could be at work in a unified, translucent consciousness that would allow one to success-fully deceive oneself in this way?

The Achievement of Bad Faith

While Sartre's account of belief allows for the possibility of self-deception, he does not explicitly account for a mechanism that might accomplish this. However, Adrian Mirvish has provided an account on Sartre's behalf, extracted from examples of bad faith in *Being and Nothingness* and drawing from principles of Gestalt psychology.[27] It is to Mirvish's account of the mechanism of bad faith that we now turn.

In *Being and Nothingness*, one finds several references to Gestalt psychology and instances in which Sartre employs Gestalt psychology's *figure-ground* analysis of perception. For example, it will be recalled from chapter 1 that there is a negation that takes place in positional consciousness of an object, such that the object is apprehended by virtue of its not being any other thing. Sartre describes this in Gestaltist terms when he writes that "we must understand indeed that *this* particular being can be called *this* only on the ground of the presence of *all* being,"[28] and that "this original relation between the all and the 'this' is at the source of the relation between figure and ground which the 'Gestalt theory' has brought to light" (182). Elsewhere Sartre writes:

> The object appears on the ground of the world and manifests itself in a relation of exteriority with other "thises" which have just appeared. Thus its revelation implies the complementary constitution of an undif-ferentiated ground which is the total perceptive field or the world. (316)

Thus we have evidence that Sartre adopted a figure-ground view of per-ception: for Sartre, we do not perceive the world as a collection of dis-crete, equally clearly apparent items; rather, the world is a relatively un-differentiated ground upon which certain, more clearly defined "thises" appear.

As a first step toward understanding how the notion of figure-ground perception may assist us in uncovering the mechanism of bad faith, let us examine an example in which, Mirvish claims, this notion comes in to play. It is a common experience among those who drive cars that they can be daydreaming, talking to a passenger, or even consulting a map while they are driving and still manage to successfully arrive at their destination. Furthermore, upon completing the journey, they may be able to recollect in some detail their imaginings or conversation and yet have little or no recollection of the series of complex maneuvers they had performed in their capacity as driver. In such a case, although the driver is not reflectively aware of her driving, this does not indicate that she is, somehow, "passively" driving. Operating a car is a complicated procedure requiring the physical co-ordination of a number of activities (such as steering, changing gears, adjusting speed, and so on) and judgments concerning the environment (the position of other cars, presence of signs and lights, road conditions, and so on). Nor is it a matter of reflex or habit (in any simple, mechanistic sense of these terms). The variables involved in driving are numerous and their ranges are extensive. So much so that, although there may be a set number of kinds of operation involved, the specifics of each maneuver (such as the exact pressure on the accelerator or brake, the precise angle of the steering wheel, the timing of each operation in relation to others and the trip as a whole, and so on) may be such that it is virtually unique. Driving requires a multitude of complex judgments made by an embodied subject operating a complicated instrument. Yet despite all of this, the subject can be engaged in some other activity at the same time, such that on the completion of the journey the subject can recall in detail this other activity, while having little recollection of how the journey was made.[29]

Mirvish relates to this type of case the notion of figure-ground. He claims that the notion of figure-ground can account for "a phenomenon in which a subject can exhibit a functionally dichotomized consciousness with two concomitant series of functionally disparate actions" (252). In the case of driving a car while thinking about something else or talking to a passenger, the thinking or talking constitutes the focus of awareness, the *figure*, as opposed to the driving, which forms (at least a part of) the *ground*.

A few points regarding figure and ground need to be raised. First, the figure is not to be understood as separate from the ground. The figure arises as a result of focusing awareness on an aspect of a field of experience. The act of focusing awareness creates both a differentiated figure and a relatively undifferentiated ground. Second, focusing on the figure will automatically lead to the relegation of the rest of the field of experience to the level of ground. Third, the relative differentiations of figure and ground admit of degrees. The more one focuses on the figure, the less differentiated becomes the ground. In the case of driving a car while thinking about something else, the more one is focused on the daydream, the less one is pre-reflectively aware of driving, which greatly increases the chances of not driving effectively.

Mirvish believes that the mechanism of bad faith can be understood as involving precisely this sort of figure-ground differential focusing (253). In bad faith, it is the evidence in support of the held belief that is the focus of awareness, which is to say, forms the figure. Evidence to the contrary is not focused on, and hence forms part of the ground of the field of experience. What is more, in bad faith the desire to maintain the belief is so strong that the emphasis of awareness on the evidence that forms the figure is particularly great. Recalling the point made above concerning the relative differentiation of figure and ground, where the degree of differentiation of the figure is inversely proportional to that of the ground, it becomes apparent how a person in bad faith can be observed to be almost blind to the evidence that conflicts with her held belief, despite being in contact with that evidence. It is important to understand that the claim here is not that differential focusing *is* bad faith. As we saw in chapter 1, all positional consciousness involves what we are now calling differential focusing. The point is rather that it is through the employment of differential focusing that bad faith is accomplished. While all differential focusing results in areas of the experiential field being less apparent than others, this need not result in bad faith. In a spirit of good faith and openness to evidence in relation to a held belief, one would not (due to not clinging so tightly to the belief) focus so strongly on evidence for the belief, such that evidence against it would become as unapparent as in bad faith. Clinging so tightly to a belief such that counterevidence ceases to play an epistemic role must be conducted within a project of bad faith. It is through this project that differential focusing becomes a tool of bad faith. All bad faith involves differential focusing, but not all differential focusing involves bad faith.

Using such an analysis in the case of the waiter, for example, the waiter can be understood to focus on those aspects of his behavior that suggest that it is somehow automatic and related to his role like a quality is related to an object. As such, the objectness of his waiter-hood forms the figure in his field of experience of himself. Concomitantly, those aspects of his behavior that refer to him as an active, creative agent form part of the undifferentiated ground of his experience. The more he focuses on the object side of his role, the less differentiated will be his experience of the subject-centered aspect of his waiterhood. For instance, it will be recalled that Sartre observes that the waiter is a little too much like a waiter, engaging in a series of exaggerated, waiter-like actions that have an air of artificiality about them. Sartre writes that "he applies himself to chaining his movements as if they were mechanisms, the one regulating the other; his gestures and even his voice seem to be mechanisms; he gives himself the quickness and pitiless rapidity of things."[30] Such a mode of behavior could be interpreted as betraying a high degree of self-consciousness concerning it. When, for instance, a patron catches the waiter's eye, the waiter's goal is not simply to go and serve the patron, but to serve her in a particular way, to serve her in the manner of a waiter-automaton. The waiter is focused on his behavior as a series of mechanisms that regulate each other and refer to each other in a deterministic manner. As such, the awareness of himself as the creative source of this behavior dissipates into the undifferentiated ground of his experience. The fact that he could ignore the patron, or deliberately spill the soup onto her lap, should he choose, forms part of the indistinct background, so that such possibilities, while present, never intrude on the waiter-object activity that is the figure of his experience. Through this differential figure-ground focusing, the waiter is able to avoid awareness of aspects of his being-in-the-world and his situation that constitute evidence contradicting his belief that he is a waiter in the mode of being-in-itself.

Bad Faith and the Translucency of Consciousness

The above account of the mechanism of bad faith can also be accommodated by Sartre's notion of the translucency of consciousness (49). Some commentators have taken Sartre's claim that consciousness is translucent to entail that self-deception would be impossible. For example, M. R. Haight takes Sartre's claim to mean "consciousness is totally translucent, so that one part can never hide its workings from another."[31] It is apparent that Haight takes Sartre to mean *transparency* when he writes *translucency*. If Sartre did mean that consciousness is totally transparent, this would seem to suggest that self-deception is impossible.[32] But is this a correct interpretation of *translucency*?

While *translucent* means allowing the passage of light, thus rendering it an antonym to *opaque*, it need not mean *transparent*. *Translucent* can refer to *transparent* or to *semi-transparent* (in the sense that frosted glass is semi-transparent).[33] Which of these senses of *translucent* does Sartre intend us to apply? Phyllis Sutton Morris argues that neither of them captures Sartre's meaning in each context.[34] However, we can be certain that he at least sometimes uses *translucent* to mean *semi-transparent*. Given the above interpretation of bad faith in terms of figure-ground differential focusing, such an approach to translucency is quite fitting. Sometimes consciousness will give a transparent view of an object (when the object is the figure) and sometimes it will give a less clear, indistinct view of the object (when the object is part of the ground of experience). Either way, we can assume that consciousness will not provide a perfectly clear view of the entire field of experience, and is thus able to "cover over" some things, making them less distinct.[35]

The figure-ground interpretation of bad faith, which Mirvish has made explicit, has the great virtue of not only allowing for the translucency of consciousness; it requires it. If consciousness were always transparent, no self-deception would be possible, as there would be no way for consciousness to hide things from itself by making them unclear through differential focusing. Nor would self-deception be possible if consciousness were opaque, as there would then be no possibility of there being a differentiated figure and an undifferentiated ground.[36] Without a ground made up of, among other things, indistinctly viewed unwelcome evidence, consciousness could only be mistaken, never self-deceived. It is only if consciousness is translucent that it would be able to make objects more or less clear and thus deceive itself through the obscuration of evidence in its midst.

Thus the figure-ground differential focusing account of bad faith is able to accommodate Sartre's views that the mind is unified (as opposed to psychoanalytic models, which hold that the mind is divided into discrete functional units) and that consciousness is translucent. But, if a bad-faith belief can be held only through averting attention away from key evidence, which is always present on the periphery of awareness, will it not be difficult to maintain the belief? How stable can bad faith beliefs be? Sartre's answer is that they are not very stable at all. He emphasizes what he calls the *evanescence* or *metastability* of bad faith:

> There is in fact an "evanescence" of bad faith, which, it is evident, vacillates continually between good faith and cynicism: Even though the existence of bad faith is very precarious, and though it belongs to the kind of psychic structures which we might call "metastable," it presents nonetheless an autonomous and durable form. It can even be the normal aspect of life for a very great number of people. A person can *live* in bad faith, which does not mean that he does not have abrupt awakenings to cynicism or to good faith, but which implies a constant and particular style of life.[37]

Bad faith beliefs are precarious. They vacillate between good faith (which would be moments in which awareness of key counterevidence has become so dim as to have effectively disappeared, in which case they are better understood in terms of error, rather than self-deception) and cynicism (in which one brings to focused attention the contrary evidence and can no longer maintain the lie). Nonetheless, people can and do live in bad faith. As there is no stable state of bad faith, living in bad faith requires constant maintenance. Bad faith beliefs are not generated and then held once and for all. Rather, they are held as part of a wider, bad faith project, which will motivate their constant fine-tuning and adjustment. As such, a person in bad faith must bear responsibility not just for a one-off epistemic indiscretion but, rather, for an entire way of life.

We have seen that bad faith has intimately related ontological and epistemic dimensions. Bad faith involves self-deceptively held beliefs about the nature of oneself and, as will become more apparent in later chapters, the nature of others. I want to claim that various forms of oppression, such as racism and sexism, can involve the oppressor holding false beliefs about himself and those that he oppresses and that, when this is so, we can interpret the holding of those beliefs (which may not be reflectively held) in terms of bad faith. As a first step toward supporting this claim, I will, in the next chapter, examine a case of oppression in which bad faith would appear to be present.

NOTES

1. Sartre, *Being and Nothingness*, 56.
2. Toril Moi translates this passage differently to Barnes, substituting "crude" for "cruel" (Moi, *Simone de Beauvoir*, 127).
3. Moi, *Simone de Beauvoir*, 127.
4. Sartre, *Being and Nothingness*, 55.
5. Moi, *Simone de Beauvoir*, 129.
6. Sartre, *Being and Nothingness*, 59. Robert D. Cumming suggests that the way in which the waiter in this example "plays" with the tray is the physical embodiment of what Sartre refers to as the *metastability* of bad faith, which will be discussed at the end of this chapter (Robert D. Cumming, "Role-Playing," 50).
7. While the homophobia that infects Sartre's example (particularly his conflation of *homosexual* and *paederast* and his references to "guilt" and "the guilty one") is offensive, this is the example that Sartre gives, and as it stands (putting offense to one side) it does provide a good illustration of the structure of the bad faith that he is considering.
8. Eric Matthews has made a similar observation. See *Twentieth-Century French Philosophy*, 70–71.
9. Mary Warnock, *Philosophy of Sartre*, 53.
10. Michèle Le Doeuff, "Operative Philosophy," 146. Elsewhere Le Doeuff claims that "bad faith . . . consists in refusing to recognize oneself as a free subject and claiming to be determined or hindered by external circumstances" (Le Doeuff, *Hipparchia's Choice*, 60).
11. Le Doeuff, "Operative Philosophy," 145.

12. Moi, *Simone de Beauvoir*, 105, emphasis added. It may be noted that in a footnote in the same work, Moi does mention transcendence in the context of bad faith. However, here she claims that "bad faith is seen . . . as the refusal to choose between facticity and transcendence" (274). To the contrary, Sartre would claim that a choice for either facticity or transcendence (if we are to understand choice as referring to an exclusive adoption of one or the other) would, either way, constitute bad faith.

13. Warnock, *Philosophy of Sartre*, 56–59.

14. Lewis Gordon, *Bad Faith and Anti-Black Racism*, 17.

15. Sartre, *Being and Nothingness*, 57.

16. Attributing to people beliefs that they have never explicitly or reflectively held seems plausible: surely, for example, we are inclined to think of most people carrying an at least implicitly learned and held metaphysics that informs their actions. Thanks to Ward Jones for this point.

17. Sartre, *Being and Nothingness*, 49.

18. Alfred R. Mele, *Irrationality*, 121.

19. There is a vast amount of literature on self-deception, and a number of approaches have been taken to the issue, but it is far beyond the scope of this book to provide an extensive coverage of these. My approach will be limited to giving an account of the possibility of self-deception in a unified consciousness that is compatible with Sartre's model of mind. An alternative, general kind of solution to the "paradox of belief" is to compartmentalize the mind into functional units containing different beliefs. This approach, made famous by (though by no means limited to) Freudian psychoanalysis, is criticized by Sartre (*Being and Nothingness*, 50–54), who claims that it provides no real solution at all. For criticisms of Sartre's argument against Freud, see Jerome Neu, "Divided Minds," and Allen W. Wood, "Self-Deception and Bad Faith." For a (limited) defense of Sartre's argument against Freud and additional criticisms of the divided-mind approach to self-deception, see Mark Johnston, "Self-Deception and the Nature of Mind."

20. Sartre, *Being and Nothingness*, 67.

21. While not a contradiction, both believing and disbelieving p may well still be the occasion for epistemic unease.

22. Wood, "Self-Deception and Bad Faith," 218. Note that "believing*" is Wood's notation for what I have been referring to as mere believing.

23. Sartre, *Being and Nothingness*, 70.

24. Joseph S. Catalano, "Successfully Lying to Oneself," 684.

25. Sartre, *Being and Nothingness*, 68.

26. In the next chapter I will examine extensively an example of bad faith in which emotion plays a crucial role in the bad faith project.

27. Adrian Mirvish, "Gestalt Mechanisms." Two other articles in which Mirvish examines the influence of Gestalt psychology on Sartre's philosophy are "Sartre and the Gestaltists" and "Sartre on Perception and the World."

28. Sartre, *Being and Nothingness*, 180.

29. Mirvish, "Gestalt Mechanisms," 250–51.

30. Sartre, *Being and Nothingness*, 59.

31. M. R. Haight, *A Study of Self-Deception*, 53–54.

32. Phyllis Sutton Morris claims that even if this were a correct interpretation of Sartre's model of consciousness, it might still be possible for his model to allow for self-deception (Morris, "Sartre on the Self-Deceiver," 105).

33. One definition of *translucent* offered in the *Oxford English Dictionary* is "Allowing the passage of light, yet diffusing it so as not to render bodies lying beyond clearly visible; semi-transparent." http://dictionary.oed.com/cgi/entry/00256351 (March 11, 2002).

34. Morris, "Sartre on the Self-Deceiver," 105.

35. Catalano holds a similar interpretation of the translucency of consciousness. He writes that "to be conscious, for Sartre is to be aware. But, and this is crucial, *this awareness does not have to be a thetic comprehension.* Sartre's claim that consciousness is translucent does not imply that we always have a correct understanding of that of which we are aware, whether this be our own internal states or external objects. Translucency does not guarantee that I will always correctly conceptualize that of which I am aware" (Catalano, "Successfully Lying to Oneself," 680). Catalano's emphasis on not all consciousness entailing thetic awareness ties in nicely with the figure-ground analysis given above, where we can understand the figure to be the object of thetic awareness.

36. Mirvish, "Gestalt Mechanisms," 254.

37. Sartre, *Being and Nothingness*, 50.

3

Anti-Semitic Racism and the Flight from Transcendence

It is my contention that Sartre's concept of bad faith can be used to provide a partial account of oppression. In the last chapter we examined Sartre's notion of bad faith, its connection with Sartre's human ontology and how it was possible, given his model of consciousness. We also discovered that there are two possible, general types of bad faith: one a denial of transcendence and/or identification with facticity, the other a denial of facticity and/or identification with transcendence. In this chapter I will examine a case of oppression, anti-Semitic racism, in which the oppressor appears to engage in the first type of bad faith. The case I will examine is one of Sartre's own; the anti-Semite described in *Anti-Semite and Jew*.

I will argue that the anti-Semite in Sartre's portrait of anti-Semitism engages in bad faith of the first type. However, from the outset I wish to stress that while the anti-Semitism Sartre describes appears as a manifestation of the first type of bad faith, it is not the case that anti-Semitism involving bad faith is necessarily tied to this particular type of bad faith. It is quite possible to conceive of another style of anti-Semitism involving the second type of bad faith: bad faith as a denial of facticity. However, in the context of *Anti-Semite and Jew*, I will claim, the bad faith of the anti-Semite is of the first type.[1]

Apart from interpreting Sartre's account of anti-Semitism in terms of bad faith, this chapter has two other purposes. First, it examines

Sartre's portrait of the anti-Semite in light of his theory of emotion. The relation between Sartre's earlier work on emotion and his account of anti-Semitism has received little attention in the literature, yet through exploring this relation a number of the insights emerging from *Anti-Semite and Jew* can be clarified and deepened. This exploration will also serve to highlight the way in which emotion may function in bad faith, and how it allows us to see that racist beliefs and attitudes need not be simply matters of faulty cognition. The second purpose of this chapter is to present for reappraisal Sartre's early views on anti-Semitism. Sartre's account of anti-Semitism is by no means an exhaustive one. As with much of Sartre's early work, *Anti-Semite and Jew* shows insufficient appreciation of the social and political dimensions of oppression. The focus is wholly on the individual and his or her responsibility for anti-Semitism. However, accepting these limitations, the account does contain some valuable insights for an understanding of contemporary racism.

ANTI-SEMITIC OPINIONS AND MANICHAEISM

One sometimes hears the claim made by racists inhabiting the populist political niche that the so-called politically correct should not attempt to stifle the expression of opinions that they (the politically correct) deem racist. It is argued that the stifling of these opinions breaches the right to freedom of speech. In *Anti-Semite and Jew*, Sartre addresses the issue of anti-Semitic opinions. He argues that framing anti-Semitism in terms of *opinion* is an erroneous step toward an understanding of the phenomenon for two reasons: first, it plays down anti-Semitism's importance and, second, it masks anti-Semitism's true role in the life of the anti-Semite. Sartre claims that designating a phenomenon as *opinion* serves to equate it with *taste*, suggesting that it is natural and, in a sense, on an equal footing with other such phenomena.[2] Opinions are often taken to arise spontaneously as effects of subjective experience. They are natural in that they arise mechanically in response to experience, rather than as fabricated components of some wider, personal agenda. They are equal in that, as naturally occurring phenomena, everyone amasses them. They are thus beyond scrutiny and debate. It is, for example, by designating conflicting positions as being matters of (mere) opinion that one can attempt to defuse a potentially acrimonious dinner party discussion.[3]

Sartre's second main point regarding opinions concerns the way in which they are often taken to relate accidentally to each other, and to the person as a totality. The designation of anti-Semitism as *opinion* deflects attention from the anti-Semite, stopping us from asking "What is it about this person that leads him to hold such beliefs?"[4] Sartre claims that just as we tend "to look at every object in an analytic spirit, that is to say, as a composite whose elements can be separated," we take opinions to be akin to the tiles that make up a mosaic, where the mosaic is the complete personality.[5] These elements are quite separable, independent of each other. They are interchangeable molecules that can combine with others without undergoing any change in themselves. Hence, Sartre writes:

> A man may be a good father and a good citizen, highly cultivated, philanthropic, *and* in addition an anti-Semite. He may like fishing and the pleasures of love, may be tolerant in matters of religion, full of generous notions on the condition of the natives in Central Africa, *and* in addition detest the Jews. (8)

As opinions are taken to be the results of one's particular experiences, they are individual accidents that reveal nothing of an underlying project of a personality, and can be discussed as inconsequential. Against this Sartre writes, "I refuse to characterize as opinion a doctrine that is aimed directly at particular persons and that seeks to suppress their rights or to exterminate them" (9). The expression of anti-Semitic opinions is not the expression of personal tastes that can be separated from other aspects of one's life and worldview. Rather it is both an indication and part of a racist project that is open to criticism.[6]

Sartre refuses to accept that anti-Semitism is a matter of opinion. Anti-Semitism, he says, is not even an idea; it is a passion.[7] As we shall see, in naming anti-Semitism a passion, Sartre wishes to draw attention back to the anti-Semite as a subject, to view him as a human totality engaged in the world and to suggest a role that such passion plays in this totality. But first, let us look at some other points that he makes about anti-Semitism being a passion.

If anti-Semitism is not a matter of taste or mere opinion, perhaps it is the result of empirical observation and rational argument. After all, anti-Semites are rarely at a loss to provide reasons for their position. Against this, Sartre claims that although the anti-Semite may appeal to ideas and justifying arguments in support of his position, these are created after the fact of the passion of anti-Semitism. Sartre provides some examples, from his own experience, of the sorts of "evidence" put forward by anti-Semites to justify their opposition to Jews. There is an actor who has had his career ruined by Jews who have confined him to minor roles, and a young woman whose fur coat was damaged by a Jewish furrier. While it may be understandable that such people feel animosity towards those who have harmed them, it still makes sense to ask why they choose to hate Jews. Why not hate directors or furriers in general? Or, better yet, why not hate this particular Jewish director or that particular Jewish furrier (11–12)?

The answer Sartre gives is that such choices to hate Jews betray a predisposition toward anti-Semitism. When statistics regarding, for example, the participation rate of Jews in the armed services are raised as evidence in support of anti-Semitism, what is most curious is not the statistics themselves, but rather the fact that someone bothered to compile and consult them (14). "Far from experience producing his idea of the Jew, it was the latter which explained his experience" (13). Again, we see the passion of anti-Semitism lying prior to, and indeed explaining, the rationalization of the position.

What is it that acts as the predisposition toward anti-Semitism? It is, Sartre claims, the style of worldview adopted by the anti-Semite, which lies behind, and results in the manifestation of, anti-Semitism. Sartre categorizes this worldview as *Manichaeism*,[8] which he explains as follows:

> Anti-Semitism is . . . at bottom a form of Manichaeism. It explains the course of the world by the struggle of the principle of Good with the principle of Evil. Between these two principles no reconciliation is conceivable; one of them must triumph and the other be annihilated. . . . [However] the anti-Semite does not have recourse to Manichaeism as a

secondary principle of explanation. It is the original choice he makes of Manichaeism which explains and conditions anti-Semitism.[9]

In adopting a Manichaean worldview, the anti-Semite sees the world as populated by beings who can be sharply categorized as either good or evil; where the anti-Semite is good and "the Jew," evil.[10]

It is not only the characteristics of personality that become tainted and evil by mere virtue of their "Jewishness." For example, "work coming from his [the Jew's] hands necessarily bears his stigma. If he builds a bridge, that bridge, being Jewish, is bad from the first to the last span."[11] Thus, Sartre suggests that material objects, constructed or touched by "a Jew," can be seen as being or becoming evil in themselves when viewed from the anti-Semite's Manichaean perspective. This extends even to the air that "the Jew" breathes and the water in which he bathes.

While we are yet to examine the anti-Semite's bad faith (this will be done in a later section of the chapter) we can already see an element of bad faith with respect to the anti-Semite's view of "the Jew." This lies in the anti-Semite's judgment that there exists a "Jewish essence." By judging that "the Jew" is essence governed, the anti-Semite interprets "the Jew" to be fixed in the in-itself. Such a judgment requires ignoring features of the actual Jewish people that the anti-Semite meets. There will surely be aspects of any actual Jewish person that will not fit with the anti-Semite's notion of "the Jew," and these will have to be ignored in order for the anti-Semite's judgment to stand.

Although Sartre claims, in the quotation above, that Manichaeism is the defining characteristic of anti-Semitism, he does refer to another metaphysical attitude assumed by Manichaeism, and without which Manichaeism could not be adopted. This is the *spirit of synthesis*. In contrast to the *analytic spirit*, which views the whole as merely the sum of its parts and which can function to defuse anti-Semitism as mere opinion, the spirit of synthesis views the whole as more than the sum of its parts. This allows the anti-Semite to hold that, for example, it is not the case that "the Jew" has a particular characteristic, such as greed or cowardice, or set of characteristics that, if removed or replaced, would make "the Jew" acceptable. The anti-Semite believes in an evil or inferior "Jewish essence," and by using the spirit of synthesis he can see that this essence stains everything connected with "the Jew." So, for example, "[the Jew's] virtues, if he has any, turn to vices by reason of the fact that they are his" (33). Both "the Jew" and "the Aryan" may have intelligence, but the former has "Jewish intelligence" as opposed to the latter's "Aryan intelligence." The same would apply to courage and cowardice, creativity and dullness.

We would do well to pause here and ask: "Is this Manichaeism, to which Sartre refers, simply an erroneous worldview?" While it would be an understatement to say that the anti-Semite's worldview is incorrect, is the anti-Semite simply mistaken, or does the anti-Semite have something to gain from a commitment to it, such that the commitment can be understood as motivated? Recall the claim that started us off in this direction: anti-Semitism is based on passion. What is now needed is an understanding of what Sartre means by *passion* and, following that, to uncover the consequences of the claim that anti-Semitism is based on passion to our understanding of anti-Semitism itself. Reference to Sartre's theory of passion (or *emotion* as he calls it in his most complete work on the subject),[12] will demonstrate that, in claiming that anti-Semitism is based on passion, Sartre holds that the anti-Semite's view of the world is intentional and goal-directed, rather than simply erroneous. This understanding of anti-Semitism as passion will help to clarify the way in which Manichaeism arises and the role that Manichaeism plays, for Sartre, in anti-Semitism. Furthermore, by interpreting anti-Semitism in terms of emotion, we will be able to see that the beliefs that the anti-Semite holds in bad faith are not simply false, not simply the result of some cognitive fault, but rather are a part of a constructed world of belief.

EMOTION AND PASSION

Sartre's Theory of Emotion and Passion

In *The Emotions: Outline of a Theory*, Sartre provides an account of emotional conduct as being intentional and an active response to a situation. Sartre's claim that emotions are intentional is characteristic of his existential phenomenological framework, which holds that all consciousness and human activity is intentional in the sense of being meaning producing and directed toward some thing in the world. Sartre's theory of emotion draws heavily on his idea of intentionality in another way. As will emerge from this section, emotion is a conscious act that *colors* the object that it intends. Here, Sartre's view that consciousness does not merely perceive its object, but also performs a role in constituting the object, comes into play.

Sartre takes his theory of emotion as an intentional conscious act to stand in contrast to the *peripheric* theories of emotion, of which Sartre names William James as a representative. The Jamesian, or James-Lange, theory holds that

> *bodily changes follow directly the perception of the exciting fact, and that our feeling of the same changes as they occur IS the emotion.* [While] common-sense says, we lose our fortune, are sorry and weep . . . the hypothesis here to be defended says that this order of sequence is incorrect, . . . and that the more rational statement is that we feel sorry because we cry.[13]

Emotion, then, according to James, consists of awareness of the physiological changes that arise in certain situations.

Sartre's first criticism of James's account of emotion concerns the nature of the physiological modifications accompanying emotion, the awareness of which, James claims, constitutes emotion. The problem Sartre identifies with this account is that these physiological modifications tend to be similar in quite different emotions, such that it would be difficult for James to differentiate between them. For example:

> The physiological modifications which correspond to anger differ only in intensity from those which correspond to joy (slightly accelerated respiratory rhythm, slight increase in muscular tonicity, extension of bio-chemical changes, arterial tension, etc.), yet anger is not more intense joy; it is something else, at least insofar as it presents itself to consciousness.[14]

However, Sartre's main criticism concerns the role in emotion that theories such as this give to consciousness. In James's model, consciousness appears only as a reflective consciousness of the changes in physiological or psychic states connected with emotion. While Sartre concedes that we can be, and often are, conscious of being in an emotional state, for example, being aware that we are afraid, this is by no means the primary role of consciousness in emotion. Fear, for example,

> is not originally consciousness *of* being afraid, any more than the perception of this book is consciousness *of* perceiving the book. Emotional consciousness is, at first, unreflective, and on this plane it can be conscious of itself only on the non-positional mode. Emotional consciousness is, at first, consciousness *of* the world. . . . The man who is afraid is afraid *of* something. (50–51)

As such, my hatred of Mr. X is not what I am focused on in hating him. While I may become thetically aware of my emotional state, it is not in this awareness that my state consists. Rather, my hatred of Mr. X is originally my way of taking him, hatefully, as an intentional object of perception and action.

While Sartre is strongly critical of James's theory of emotion as consciousness of physiological change, it should not then be thought that Sartre dismisses the role of the body in emotion. For one, Sartre holds that the physiological changes that occur in emotion are crucial to genuine emotion, a point we will examine in detail a little later. Another role that is played by the body in Sartre's theory of emotion concerns the nature of the subject engaged in emotion, for it is the conscious subject as embodied agent in the world that lies at the heart of Sartre's model of emotion as an active response to a situation. It is this role of the body that we shall now examine.

The embodied subject carries projects with it into the world of objects and others. The world appears as unrealized possibilities. What is more, the world is instrumental. Unrealized possibilities can be realized through the application of procedures that comply with the way in which the world works. Gregory McCulloch offers the example of a bottle of soft drink.[15] It is my bottle, I am thirsty, and I have a bottle opener. The bottle appears in terms of its possibilities toward my ends. It is the bottle to be held in a certain way, acted upon with the help of the opener, opened, raised to the lips, and its contents consumed. By acting in accordance with the way the world works, I can achieve my goal of having a drink.

While the world can appear to the subject in terms of possible means to ends, pathways to our goals, it is not always encountered as such a compliant field of action. Sometimes the world can appear difficult. What is more, Sartre claims, the difficulty is apprehended directly as a quality of the world:

> This notion of difficulty is not a reflective notion which would imply a relationship to me. It is there, on the world; it is a quality of the world which is given in the perception (exactly like the paths toward the potentialities and the potentialities themselves and the exigencies of objects: books having to be read, shoes having to be assembled, etc.).[16]

To return to the example of the bottle of soft drink: I am trying to open the bottle, but despite my best attempts it will not open. Instead of appearing as a path to a goal, the bottle appears as an obstacle. The world has become difficult. My conduct toward the bottle becomes emotional. The bottle appears stupid, recalcitrant. I start talking to it, first advising it, then pleading with it, and then threatening it before I finally throw it on the floor. Given my project of having a drink, my behavior has been less than conducive. What is going on here? Sartre claims that emotional conduct such as this involves a transformation of the world:

> When the paths traced out become too difficult, or when we see no path, we can no longer live in so urgent and difficult a world. All the ways are barred. However, we must act. So we try to change the world, that is, to live as if the connection between things and their potentialities were not ruled by deterministic procedures, but by magic. (58–59)

On Sartre's use of the term "magic," Hazel Barnes writes:

> The essential point here is that the subject believes in the efficacy of the transformation—at least at the time and nonreflectively. Just as in magical practice, what matters is the agent's attitude and relation to the world at which this action is supposedly directed. The term "magical," as Sartre employs it, is more than a colorful expression. . . . Consciousness acts as if an objective transformation is taking place when, in fact, it is not.[17]

Given Sartre's account, my anger at the bottle can be interpreted as involving a transformation of the world. The world of ordinary cause and effect was resisting and disallowing the achievement of my goal and so I changed it into a new world in which objects might respond to verbal threats and corporal punishment. The transformation is not of *the* world but of *my* world. The emotional conduct is ineffective in attaining my goal, but it allows me to pursue my project for a little longer, albeit on the magical plane.

Sartre stresses that this entry into the magical is an *activity* of consciousness and not simply the result of a causal process. In order to highlight this, Sartre compares his theory of emotion with that of one of his predecessors, Pierre Janet. According to Sartre, Janet holds that when faced with a difficult situation a subject may be seen to respond with *superior behavior* that is appropriate to that situation, taking the difficulty head on, but that incurs the cost of psychological tension. Alternatively, the subject may be seen to respond with *inferior behavior* that avoids or diminishes the difficulty of the situation, behavior that is less appropriate to the situation, but that gains for the subject a lowering of psychological tension. Sartre writes: "When the task is too difficult and we cannot maintain the superior behavior which would be suitable to it, the psychic energy liberated is spent in another way: we maintain an inferior behavior which requires a lesser psychological tension."[18] Janet's theory holds that emotion is a degraded or inferior form of behavior that arises from a *setback*, that is, an obstacle that prevents or frustrates the achievement of a goal.

That there are broad similarities between the approaches to emotion taken by Janet and Sartre is clear. However, while Sartre adopts Janet's notion of emotion arising in the face of a setback, he is strongly critical of Janet's evaluation of emotion as an automatic mechanism. Janet believes that in the face of difficulty, setback behavior will automatically replace superior behavior. This would mean that instating emotion is a matter of reflex, making the subject a passive sufferer of emotion. However, Sartre believes that, by holding this, Janet misses the significance of his own insight that emotion is *setback behavior*. By denying any role in emotion to an evaluating consciousness, for which behavior can be superior or inferior, the idea of emotional behavior as setback behavior becomes incomprehensible. Sartre writes:

> If we consider the individual as a system of behavior, and if derivation occurs automatically, the setback is nothing; it does not exist; there is simply substitution of one behavior by a diffuse ensemble of organic

manifestations. For emotion to have the psychic signification of a set-back, consciousness must intervene and confer this signification upon it. It must keep the superior behavior as a possibility and must grasp the emotion precisely as a setback *in relation* to this superior behavior. (28–29)

Sartre claims that what Janet's theory of emotion lacks is an account of the finality, that is, the goal-oriented nature of emotion (28).[19] While for Janet emotional behavior is a disorder that arises automatically when superior behavior becomes difficult, for Sartre "emotional behavior is not a disorder at all. It is an organized system of means aiming at an end" (32).

An example from Janet, cited by Sartre, serves to demonstrate the difference between the two interpretations of emotional behavior. A young woman comes to Janet, wishing to confide in him the dark secret that she does not want to act as nurse to her sick father. However, when Janet provides her with the opportunity to divulge this secret she begins to sob violently. Janet interprets this sobbing as the result of her difficulty in admitting to him what her problem is (due perhaps to the shame attached to it), that is, she sobs because she is unable to say anything. The saying behavior, which would incur greater psychological tension, is automatically replaced with the inferior, but less psychological tension inducing, crying behavior. However, Sartre interprets this incident quite differently. Rather than the sobbing resulting causally from the woman's inability to speak, Sartre holds that the woman uses the sobbing to avoid speaking. He asks rhetorically "does she sob *because* she cannot say anything . . . or does she sob precisely *in order not to say anything?*" (31). While Janet's interpretation presents emotion as the passive, causal result of a difficult situation, Sartre presents emotion as goal-directed behavior.

Although he presents emotion as goal-directed behavior, it must be stressed that, for Sartre, emotion is not simply a matter of enacting a certain mode of behavior. Emotion also involves the physiological participation of the body. This is the further role in emotion that Sartre gives to the body that was mentioned earlier, and this role becomes clear when we consider his account of false emotion. If, for example, I receive a gift that I am not particularly excited about, "it is possible that I may make an external show of intense joy, that I may clap my hands, that I may jump, that I may dance. However, all this is a comedy. I shall let myself be drawn into it a little, and it would be inexact to say that I *am not* joyful. However my joy is not real" (72). In other words, I can go through the motions of emotional behavior, but this is not to be genuinely in an emotional state. True emotion is accompanied by physiological phenomena, such as hypertension and vasoconstriction. Sartre claims that in emotion the body is used "as a means of incantation" (70) and that it is the physiological phenomena constituting the incantation that "represent the *seriousness* of the emotion; they are phenomena of belief" (74). In true emotion one accomplishes the entry to the magical through the body. So, we must not consider emotion

> simply as being enacted; it is not a matter of pure demeanor. It is the demeanor of a body which is in a certain state; the state alone would not provoke the demeanor; the demeanor without the state is comedy; but the emotion appears in a highly disturbed body which retains a certain behavior. . . . We are really dealing with a synthetic form; *in order to believe* in magical behavior it is necessary to be highly disturbed. (74–75)[20]

Thus we can see that the body contributes to the believability of the magical transformation.

A further consequence of the role of the body in true emotion is that it serves to highlight a sense in which emotion *is* something undergone or suffered. We saw earlier that in order for emotion to be believable and for the magical transformation to be lived, consciousness uses the self, in particular the body, as a tool. Thus, in emotion one is *affected*. Should one reflect on one's emotional conduct, such emotion would appear to be something undergone, something that happens to one, something that one suffers. And, indeed, if emotion is genuine, one does suffer it. However, this reflection upon emotion may identify *the object*, rather than consciousness, as the source of the affect. When this happens, emotion appears to the subject as *passion*. In passion, one experiences one's emotion as something forced upon one by the object, and given the nature of emotion, this is understandable. In emotion, consciousness colors the object. For example, recall what was said earlier about the difficulty of the world. Sartre wrote that the difficulty was experienced as being there in the world.

He stressed that the "notion of difficulty is not a reflective notion which would imply a relationship with me" (58). In other words, the difficulty is not experienced as an interpretation of the world by consciousness (even though, upon reflection, it should be), but rather the difficulty is out there, in the world. The same is true for other emotional interpretations. In the example of the soft drink bottle, it is the bottle itself that is experienced as having the qualities of recalcitrance or malice, in a way analogous to its having a certain size and shape, even though in fact it is consciousness that has posited the bottle in this way. It is the bottle's recalcitrance that makes me angry, though in reality *I* have made the bottle recalcitrant. Passion is a reflection upon emotion that mistakenly identifies the object as the source of the emotion.

This is an important point to raise in the context of our present purposes. In *Anti-Semite and Jew*, Sartre speaks of anti-Semitism in terms of passion, whereas in *The Emotions* he provides a theory of emotion. In drawing together these works, as I shall do, the relationship between passion and emotion needs to be stressed. While passion and emotion are not identical, they are clearly closely related. Emotion is an act of the pre-reflective consciousness, and passion is a reflection on emotion that interprets the emotion erroneously as being caused by something outside of consciousness. Sartre claims that it is quite common to experience emotion as passion through reflection:

> Ordinarily, we direct upon the emotive consciousness an accessory reflection which certainly perceives consciousness as consciousness, but insofar as it is motivated by the object: "I am angry *because* it is hateful." It is on the basis of this reflection that the passion will constitute itself. (91)

However, emotion is not "a passive disorder of the organism and the mind which comes *from the outside* to disturb the psychic life" (90). Hence the judgment that the emotion is caused by something from the outside is, given Sartre's model, incorrect. What is experienced as passion (something thrust upon one by an object, and thus an experience in keeping with the traditional usage of *passion*, with its connotations of passivity), is in fact emotion (an *act* of consciousness). Thus, no understanding of what Sartre might mean by *passion* is possible without reference to *emotion*, and so I am justified in employing Sartre's theory of emotion in discussing the significance of his use of *passion* in *Anti-Semite and Jew.*

Criticisms of Sartre's Theory

Before moving on to a discussion of Sartre's account of anti-Semitism in light of his theory of emotion, we would do well to examine some of the problems with his theory. In particular I wish to consider three concerns raised by Joseph Fell regarding aspects of Sartre's theory of emotion that are difficult to reconcile with everyday observations of emotion.[21] These are:

1. Emotional conduct is understood by Sartre to operate with no reference to the instrumentality of the "real" (as opposed to magically transformed) world, and so should be considered wholly uninstrumental.[22]
2. Even mild emotions must be interpreted as occurring wholly on the magical plane.
3. Seemingly *positive emotions*, such as joy and love, as opposed to *negative emotions*, such as anger and fear, must be understood as responses to setbacks experienced in an all-too-difficult world.

I will address each of these in turn.

Emotion and Instrumental Action

As we have seen, Sartre claims that emotion involves a magical transformation of the world. However, Sartre can be interpreted as saying, not simply that the magical transformation of the world results in the introduction of magical elements to the instrumental world, but that it involves a complete replacement of the instrumental world with the magical. The following passages from *The Emotions* stand as evidence for this *all-or-nothing* thesis, which maintains that one operates entirely *either* on the magical plane *or* on the instrumental plane:

> *All* emotions . . . make a same world appear, a world which is cruel, terrible, gloomy, joyful, etc., but one in which the relationship of things to consciousness is *always and exclusively magical.*[23]

There is emotion when the world of instruments abruptly vanishes and the magical world appears in its place. (90)

In Fell's opinion, Sartre does hold the all-or-nothing view of the magical plane suggested by the above passages.[24] This, Fell believes, leads further to Sartre holding that on the magical plane one cannot act instrumentally. Evidence for this can be found in *The Emotions* where Sartre states that emotional behavior "is not *effective*."[25]

Claiming that emotion involves entry to a magical plane is one thing, but claiming further that this means that one is unable to act instrumentally at all is quite another. What is more, it is puzzling. Entry to the magical may alter my way of going about things but it need not be totally uninstrumental. For example, I am trying to open the drawer of my filing cabinet but cannot. I may get angry at it and start calling it names, but this does not mean that I stop pulling on the drawer in such a way that it might, in accordance with the rules of instrumentality, open. Certainly, talking to the drawer does not help in the achievement of the goal, but pulling on the drawer does. The talking indicates that I must be operating in a magically transformed world, yet I am still able to act instrumentally.

Sartre's apparent commitment to the principle that no emotional behavior is instrumental can seem to lead him at times to unusual conclusions. Take for example his account of active fear in which one flees, say, a ferocious beast:

> The flight into active fear is mistakenly considered as rational behavior. We do not flee in order to take shelter; we flee for lack of power to annihilate ourselves in the state of fainting. Flight is a fainting which is enacted; it is a magical behavior which consists of denying the dangerous object with our whole body. (63)

Describing the act of running away from a source of danger in terms of fainting (or an inability to faint) is most curious indeed. It seems clear that, in the context of a dangerous situation, the act of fleeing the source of danger is instrumental. Sartre admits that such behavior can appear to be rational: "Calculation is seen in such behavior— quick calculation to be sure—the calculation of someone who wants to put the greatest possible distance between himself and danger. But this is to misunderstand such behavior, which would then be only prudence" (63).[26] He seems to be committed to the view that if I were to identify something as a source of potential danger and then try to engage in activities that result in distance being put between myself and that thing, the activity should be interpreted differently, with regard to its instrumentality, depending on whether or not I am afraid of the object. In short, if I am not afraid of the object, my running away is instrumental, whereas if I am afraid, my running away should be interpreted as uninstrumental, that is, an ineffective mode of behavior based on delusion. However, if one were to identify something as a source of danger, it is not apparent that the presence or absence of fear should determine whether or not running away from the source of danger should be interpreted as instrumental activity. It just seems sensible to interpret it as instrumental in both cases. Even if one were to unreasonably identify something (say, a teddy bear) as a source of potential danger, *given* this identification (as contrary to rules of instrumentality as this judgment may be) running away from it could still be interpreted as an instrumental act. Sartre appears to be compelled in this direction because of the extreme thesis that one is on *either* the magical *or* the instrumental plane. This extremism leads to the next criticism.

Mild Emotions

While Sartre's account of emotion as a total flight from the instrumental in the face of a setback may seem appropriate in describing, say, a fit of rage, it would seem, on the face of it, to preclude the possibility of weaker emotions. After all, we may sometimes fly into fits of rage or faint through abject fear, but we also experience weaker emotional states such as annoyance or mild apprehension and, given this, a theory of emotion should be able to account for these milder states.

Sartre does refer to two types of mild emotion: *delicate emotion* and *weak emotion*. In delicate emotion, the subject is faced with an obstacle, but the threat it poses is not imminent and is thus only "dimly seen." "The disaster is total—we know it—it is profound; but as far as today is concerned, we catch only an imperfect glimpse of it" (82). In delicate emotion an obstacle is perceived as "total disaster" but, due to its remoteness, it does not warrant a complete transformation of the world. In weak emotion, Sartre tells us that the "affective grasp of the object is slight" (82). In other words, in weak emotion an obstacle is taken to be a minor threat: only a bit horrible, for example. This is in contrast to delicate emotion where the obstacle is very horrible, but remote. Like delicate emotions, however, weak emotions do not involve a complete transformation of the world.

The admission by Sartre of weak and delicate emotions into his account contradicts the extreme thesis, which he seems to run elsewhere, that emotion involves a total magical transformation of the world. Rather, the existence of weak and delicate emotions opens up the possibility that there can be *degrees* of magical transformation. Accepting such degrees of magical transformation would appear to be quite appropriate, given Sartre's account of emotion as a response to a situation. Different situations will warrant different responses, and it makes sense to postulate that the degree of response will be proportional to the degree of threat. However, this would necessitate giving up the all-or-nothing thesis, which regards the instrumental and magical worlds as mutually exclusive.

But must Sartre be understood to hold the all-or-nothing view of the magical plane that has been attributed to him? While there is evidence that Sartre does hold the extreme view, there exists an interesting passage in *The Emotions* that might allow for a more moderate thesis concerning the magical and instrumental worlds. Sartre writes that emotion "is possible only in an act of consciousness which destroys all the structures of the world which might *reject* the magical and reduce the event to its proper proportions" (87). While Fell interprets this passage as further evidence of the mutual exclusivity of the magical and instrumental worlds,[27] I believe that it can be interpreted as allowing for some instrumentality. It seems to allow for instrumental activity so long as that activity does not "reduce the event to its proper proportions." Thus, in the example of running away from an object of fear, the running could be viewed as instrumental even though the person is in an emotional state and so inhabiting the magical world. The magical transformation of the world in emotion will only discount the possibility of instrumental conduct that will contradict or render unbelievable the magical transformation.

It would also seem open to Sartre to allow that behavior conducted on the magical plane may have non-magical, instrumental effects. In the case of running away out of fear, for example, the fact that the running is conducted on the magical plane does not preclude the possibility that it has instrumental side effects. Thus while the running away could then be seen as motivated by the lack of power to faint, it may also happen to have the instrumental effect of placing distance between the subject and the object of their fear.

By rejecting the all-or-nothing thesis (if, indeed, Sartre holds it), we are better able to accommodate the presence of clearly instrumental activity in even vehement emotion, and the existence of delicate and weak emotions. However, Sartre's theory also runs into difficulty when we consider his account of positive emotions.

Positive Emotions

Along with emotions such as anger and fear, emotions that we might term *negative*, individuals also undergo *positive* emotions such as joy and happiness. Due to his setback model of emotion, Sartre must interpret positive emotions as involving some negative state of affairs. In joy, for example, the object of the emotion is affectively grasped as something good or desirable. So where is the setback? For Sartre, the setback lies in the fact that the object cannot be experienced all at once: "Even if the longed-for friend appears on the platform of the station, still it is an object which only yields itself little by little."[28] The project in relation to which the object (in this case, the longed-for friend) stands is the project of possessing the object now. Sartre conceives joy as a response to the frustration of being unable to achieve this. "Joy is a magical behavior which tends by incantation to realize the possession of the desired object as instantaneous totality" (69).

Thus, Sartre presents even positive emotions as involving frustration and failure. It may be plausible to suggest that, at least sometimes, joy and love can involve, perhaps even be motivated or strengthened by, fear of loss, vulnerability, and so on. In such cases perhaps joy and love could be interpreted as modes of escape from difficulty. But how plausible is this as an account of positive emotions in general? If anger and fear are generated in response to a setback that thwarts a project, surely emotions such as joy, at least sometimes, are responses to the success or coming to fruition of a project. Sartre recognizes that this can be so, but in such cases he simply refuses to accept that such joy is an emotion. Rather, he claims, it is a "feeling" that "represents a balance, an adapted state" (68). With his account of emotions as misadaptation, Sartre simply defines away the possibility of emotions that do not involve setbacks.[29]

It is the setback model of emotion that compels Sartre to treat positive emotions in this way, and this in turn draws into question the theory's ability to cover all of the phenomena that are commonly classified as emotion. Fell argues plausibly that this aspect of Sartre's theory is a result, at least in part, of its indebtedness to the work of Tamara Dembo, who aimed at describing anger in particular, rather than emotion in general.[30] This could explain why Sartre's description of emotion as involving a magical transformation of the world in response to a setback fits well with observations of some emotions, vehement anger in particular, but less well in cases of other emotions.

The foregoing criticisms of Sartre's theory of emotion are not intended to undermine Sartre's theory altogether, but rather to suggest some alterations and display its limitations. The thesis that the movement toward the magical that occurs in emotion is absolute and discounts the possibility of instrumental action (if indeed Sartre is committed to such a thesis) should be modified to allow for the possibility of the occurrence of instrumental activity in even vehement emotion. Such a modification would also serve to accommodate the occurrence of delicate and weak emotions, something that Sartre himself wanted. It should also be accepted that Sartre's theory is more applicable to some emotions than others. Thus Sartre's theory appears as an ingenious and plausible account of vehement emotions engaged in the face of obstacles, but seems less appropriate in accounting for emotions such as happiness that do not involve an obstacle to success but an instance of success.

BAD FAITH, PASSION, AND ANTI-SEMITISM

Sartre's account of passion/emotion maintains that passionate/emotional conduct is an active response to a situation that involves a magical transformation of an all-too-difficult world, a world that thwarts us in our aims, into a new world made more congenial through the removal of the normal constraints of instrumentality and determinism. Given this account of passion in conjunction with Sartre's claim that anti-Semitism is based on passion, we can interpret the anti-Semite's Manichaeism as one such magical transformation of the world. Through this interpretation we can infer that the anti-Semite's passion, and his concomitant adoption of the Manichaean attitude, is a response to some situation of elemental frustration and ineffectuality.

The question to ask now is "What is it that the anti-Semite is experiencing difficulty with?" or "How is the anti-Semite being thwarted by the way the world is, such that he should seek to change it, desperately, as in magic, and, finally, violently so as to destroy the whole existential structure of the problem?" Sartre's answer lies in the claim that "anti-Semitism, in short, is a fear of the human condition."[31] The "human condition" to which Sartre refers here is, as we have seen, the predicament that all humans face in at once participating in two modes of being: being-for-itself and being-in-itself. While Sartre thinks it possible to coordinate these two aspects of human being, he claims that, instead, one often resorts to bad faith. We saw in chapter 2 that there are two general types of bad faith: one involving the denial of transcendence, the other a denial of facticity. Which of these two types is evident in the case of the anti-Semite? The following passage makes the answer clear:

> In adopting anti-Semitism, he does not simply adopt an opinion, he chooses himself as a person. He chooses the permanence and impenetrability of stone, the total irresponsibility of the warrior who obeys his leaders—and he has no leader. He chooses to acquire nothing, to deserve nothing; he assumes that everything is given him as his birthright—and he is not noble. He chooses finally a Good which is fixed once and for all, beyond question, out of reach; he dares not examine it for fear of being led to challenge it and having to seek it in another form. (53–54)

The bad faith described in the passage is a flight toward givenness and permanence. This identifies the bad faith at issue as involving identification with facticity and denial of transcendence. The values of the anti-Semite are "fixed once and for all, beyond question," and the anti-Semite's identity has "the permanence and impenetrability of stone." There is no room for freedom and transcendence in the anti-Semite's view of himself, or his view of others and the world. The anti-Semite is frightened by the human condition. Most particularly, the anti-Semite is frightened by his own freedom, which if recognized, would demand responsibility on his part. The flight into bad faith is achieved through the passionate response to the anti-Semite's situation, which generates a new, Manichaean world that can better sustain the escape from freedom and responsibility.

Reference to the bad faith of anti-Semitism assists us toward an understanding of Sartre's position on the spirit of synthesis. We saw earlier in this chapter that in discussing anti-Semitism, Sartre refers to a synthetic spirit, which he contrasts with the analytic spirit often employed in the description of an attitude in terms of mere opinion. While the synthetic spirit takes a whole to be "more and other than the sum of its parts" (34), the analytic spirit takes "every object . . . as a composite whose elements can be separated" (8). Sartre claims that the anti-Semite adopts the synthetic spirit, and that this underpins the anti-Semite's Manichaean judgment that there exists an evil "Jewish essence" that infects everything (attributes, personality, even material objects) connected with "the Jew."[32] Which of these spirits, the analytic or synthetic, does Sartre himself adopt? As it happens, Sartre adopts a synthetic spirit, but for a very different purpose. For Sartre, the human subject, as being-for-itself, can surpass, move beyond, its former self. In propelling itself into an undetermined future, the human subject can change itself, reinterpret its situation and facticity, and give new meaning and significance to all things. In short, the spirit of synthesis is intimately connected to Sartre's fundamental notion of the subject as a free, human totality that surpasses any simple addition of its raw elements. But this stands in stark contrast to the anti-Semite's employment of the spirit of synthesis. The anti-Semite's "synthesis" involves coloring any quality possessed by a Jewish person as "essentially Jewish." So, to the anti-Semite, the value and meaning of the people he abhors are far from dynamic. To the anti-Semite, the value and meaning of "being Jewish" and of Jews themselves are ossified, permanent. The Manichaeism of the anti-Semite puts a small set of fixed values and meanings in place, such as the goodness of the fatherland and of those who spring from its soil as opposed to the evil of "the Jew," and interprets people deterministically in light of them. Thus the notion of a person as a synthetic whole, which in Sartre's hands is used to *highlight* freedom, is used by the anti-Semite to discount the possibility of change, to *ignore* freedom. "The Jew," through possession of "the Jewish essence," is destined to commit evil. But it is not just the freedom of "the Jew" that is thus ignored. The anti-Semite is able similarly to ignore his own freedom, which indeed he must do in order to live in his brand of bad faith.

Sartre's account in *Anti-Semite and Jew* of the anti-Semite in bad faith found earlier expression in his short story "The Childhood of a Leader." Here, Sartre traces Lucien Fleurier's search in childhood and adolescence for an identity. Lucien first grapples with the identity given to him by his parents and other adults before experimenting with identities gleaned from psychoanalysis and surrealism. Finally, he rejects these in favor of anti-Semitism. The crisis of Lucien's earlier searching is symbolized by his wish to have direct access to his own back: "[Lucien] touched his back and regretted not being another person to be able to caress his own flesh like a piece of silk."[33] After embracing the identity of the anti-Semite, Lucien

> suddenly forgot the Source [the café he is sitting in] and the dagos, he only saw a back, a wide back hunched with muscles going farther and farther away, losing itself, implacable, in the fog. . . . Lucien was flooded with an almost intolerable joy: this powerful, solitary back was *his own*. (216)

What is the significance of being able to see one's own back in this context? Interpreted from a temporal perspective, this can be understood as seeing oneself in the future, from the point of view of the present. It is as if Lucien is already in the future; he must be there because he can see his own back. The present Lucien can see a detailed image of the future Lucien that lies ahead of him. He knows what he will be. Lucien is in bad faith by virtue of rejecting the openness of his future that is entailed by his freedom, and thereby fleeing toward the in-itself. While we might call this scene, in which he sees his own back, a "vision," we should not think of it as purely imaginary spectacle. It is more than Lucien simply *wondering* about what he might be like. It betrays his *decision* to not change, to not be free.

In connection with this, the metaphor of seeing one's own back also refers to the idea of existing all at once. In *Anti-Semite and Jew*, Sartre writes:

> The rational man groans as he gropes for the truth; he knows that his reasoning is no more than tentative, that other considerations may supervene to cast doubt on it. He never sees very clearly where he is going; he is "open." . . . But there are people who are attracted by the durability of stone. They wish to be massive and impenetrable; they wish not to change. . . . They want to exist all at once and right away. They do not want any acquired opinions; they want them to be innate. Since they are afraid of reasoning, they wish to lead the kind of life wherein reasoning and research play only a subordinate role, wherein one seeks only what he has already found, wherein one becomes only what he already was.[34]

To be able to see one's own back is to be able to see oneself from all possible perspectives. As such, one must, in a sense, already be there, ahead of time. This permanence is the permanence of bad faith, in particular that type of bad faith characterized by a denial of transcendence. It presupposes a stasis of identity, an objectness of identity, such that Lucien *is* an anti-Semite in the way that a table *is* a table. By seeing his identity as fixed, innate, and determined by the soil of his birthplace, he need never question it again. There is to be no more of the dynamic, grueling movement into the future. With a fixed identity he is already there, he has arrived, and he has a clear picture of himself as he will always be.

I have been suggesting (in light of the claim that anti-Semitism is a passion in conjunction with Sartre's theory of emotion) that the anti-Semite's Manichaeism can be interpreted as involving a magical transformation of the world. But what about the anti-Semite's fear of freedom/transcendence: how does that fit into the interpretation of anti-Semitism as involving passion?

It might be argued that living in freedom itself stands as a frustrated project. Has the anti-Semite tried to live in freedom and found it too difficult? Whatever the origin, the present character of the anti-Semite's behavior is to transform magically an all-too-difficult part of the world that thwarts the pursuit of some more specific goal. The pursuit of a project requiring freedom and responsibility could always be frustrated, and one may engage in an emotional response to that frustration. The general solution, which would protect one in advance from all frustration stemming from or related to one's freedom, is to remove not only the specific intransigent object, but also freedom itself from the ontology of one's magically transformed world. If so the role of freedom in the anti-Semite's project turns out to run parallel with the role of the world's instrumentality, as in the simple project of opening a bottle of drink. The soft drink bottle cannot be opened by the normal procedures used to remove the cap and the response is to seek to alter the world such that normal instrumentality no longer applies. The anti-Semite's project cannot be pursued easily in accordance with freedom, and the response is to alter the world so that freedom is ignored. In the anti-Semite's Manichaean world of "good Aryans" and "evil Jews" there is no place for freedom.

And what of the project in which the anti-Semite is engaged, the obstruction of which his emotional conduct is an attempt to overcome? In trying to drink from a soft drink bottle that cannot be opened, the bottle becomes the object of my emotion. I want to open the bottle, cannot do so, and then proceed to express anger toward the bottle. In anti-Semitism it is "the Jew" that is the target of hatred, but "the Jew" (a particular Jewish people or some group of people considered as "the Jewish people") is not the separate force outside the anti-Semite that propels him into anti-Semitism. As Sartre argues, the anti-Semite's Manichaeism exists prior to the anti-Semite's designation of "the Jew" as evil. But what project would be involved on the part of a budding anti-Semite? I suggest that there need be no one project that all proto-anti-Semites share, the obstruction of which motivates them to anti-Semitic passion. There need be no single project simply because it is not the *project* that anti-Semites share, but rather the *response* to a frustrated project, whatever project that may be, which unites them.

Take for example two projects: becoming an academic and obtaining a bank loan. Both involve interplay between transcendence and the facticity of the situation. The facticity involved in becoming an academic might include such past actions or events as degrees awarded, papers published, and people met, along with present conditions to do with job availability and required areas of expertise. The role of transcendence might include such things as the presentation of past achievements to prospective employers, publishing new papers, broadening one's area of expertise, willingness to relocate, and so on. In the case of obtaining a bank loan the facticity might include one's work history, financial history, and accrual of assets, while the role of transcendence would include constructing a good case for the loan to present to the bank manager, perhaps taking on a part-time job to increase one's ability to repay the debt, and so on. Transcendence clearly plays a role in each of these projects. However, should the fulfillment of one of these projects be obstructed in some way, one may seek to alter one's perception of the situation such that it becomes one in which the role of transcendence is diminished. For example, in either of the two scenarios one could include one's racial or national origins, along with the racial or national origins of the bank manager or prospective employer, as significant aspects of the facticity of the situation, and cast these as determining elements.[35] This is what Sartre's anti-Semite does. The anti-Semite would view his failure to get the lectureship not as resulting from his lack of experience or demonstrated ability, but because the university is run by "Jews." Similarly, the anti-Semite would cast the rejection of his loan application not as being the result of his current financial position or ability to repay the loan, but rather because the bank is "Jewish." Although the two projects differ in a number of respects, it can be seen that the response in both cases is quite similar. It involves recasting the situation, magically transforming the world, into one in which racial essences determine outcomes, and it is this that Sartre's anti-Semites have in common, whoever they are. Thus it is the type of response to a frustrated project, rather than the project, that is shared by anti-Semites.

Different failures will propel different anti-Semites into their anti-Semitism. In accepting this, we can better account for the diversity of anti-Semites. It would be insufficient to refer simply to, say, white racists from lower socioeconomic groups who may experience themselves as being on the bottom of what they consider to be their pile, and assume that we have accounted for anti-Semitism in a wider sense. It is clear from Sartre's examples that he takes anti-Semitism to cut across boundaries of class, gender, and level of education. Anti-Semitism appears also in the boardroom, the gentlemen's club, and the university. By maintaining that it is the type of response to a situation that is definitive of anti-Semitism, rather than the initial situation, we will improve our chances of providing a broader account of the phenomenon.

However, despite having claimed that it is the type of response to the thwarting of a project rather than the project that anti-Semites share, the shared response reveals that there is a shared project that overarches and informs the individual projects of individual anti-Semites. The anti-Semites engage in the same type of bad faith, characterized by a flight toward the in-itself. This project of bad faith will be structurally similar in the cases of different anti-Semites, despite the fact that each individual's particular and immediate project and situation (living in a particular neighborhood, trying to become wealthy, pursuing a particular career, and so on) may be quite different in each case.

Sartre's account of anti-Semitism is an account of a structured response to the world. Particularly through reference to Sartre's theory of emotion, we can see the anti-Semite's belief in a world of moral and racial determinism as a resort to magic. However, in saying this we should not doubt that the anti-Semite actually believes in his Manichaean worldview. This is not a game. The magically transformed world is his world. But neither is the anti-Semite simply mistaken, as one might be if one happened to believe that two plus three equals six. Manichaeism plays an integral role in the anti-Semite's structured response to a difficult world.

It emerged through the discussion of bad faith beliefs in chapter 2 that while one may call on or adopt beliefs in order to integrate evidence, beliefs may also be called on or adopted in relation to other factors. Hopes and desires, for example, may motivate the adoption of beliefs. We have seen in this chapter that emotion too can play a role in the adoption or shaping of beliefs. The magically transformed world, generated through emotion, may require the adoption of beliefs that contradict available evidence in order for that world to remain consistently believable. Thus, in the case of the anti-Semite's Manichaean world, aspects of actual Jewish people that contradict the anti-Semite's portrait of "the Jew" will need to be ignored.

In the analysis of bad faith conducted in chapter 2, it was claimed that bad faith, considered in its epistemic dimensions, involves selective focusing: focusing on evidence or aspects of the world that support the beliefs held in bad faith, and ignoring or pushing out to the periphery of the experiential field aspects that contradict those beliefs. How does the anti-Semite's route to bad faith through his emotional response to the world fit with the figure-ground differential focusing mechanism considered in chapter 2? The answer would appear to be that it fits very well. It will be recalled that emotion involves a magical transformation of a difficult world. This transformation can be interpreted as involving the holding of particular, embodied beliefs. It is through such beliefs that the transformation takes place. These beliefs (such as the belief that inanimate objects can turn on you) are held not for epistemic, but rather, non-epistemic reasons. They are held as an attempt to escape the difficulty of the world, not because they strike the subject as possibly objective facts. In other words, these beliefs that are held about the world, and that constitute the transformed world, are held in a manner similar to some of the mere beliefs that were referred to earlier in chapter 2. As the subject in emotion has access to evidence that contradicts her worldview, such evidence must be rendered ineffectual, lest it disrupt the transformed world. It is quite plausible to suggest that the figure-ground differential focusing mechanism of bad faith is at work in emotion, as described by Sartre, and to further suggest that it can be seen how such emotion and bad faith can be connected.

There is another link between Sartre's theory of emotion and his account of anti-Semitism that is worth pointing out. It will be recalled that in his theory of emotion, Sartre stresses the importance of physiological phenomena in constituting the seriousness or believability of emotion. This passionate aspect of emotion also finds recognition in Sartre's portrait of the anti-Semite. Sartre claims that anti-Semitism can involve bodily modifications, such as physical discomfort and nausea. ("You see, there must be *something* about the Jews; they upset me physically."[36]) But the physical disgust for "the Jew" is not something directly caused by a Jewish person. It only comes about when the individual *believes* that the other is "a Jew." What is more, this type of reaction parallels that reserved for different others, such as "Blacks" and "Asians" (11), in different places, indicating that it is culturally relative and so further supports the thesis that any physiological changes that occur are mediated by the subject. Sartre concludes:

> Thus, it is not from the body that the sense of repulsion arises, since one may love a Jewess very well if one does not know what her race is; rather it is something that enters the body from the mind. It is an involvement of the mind, but one so deep-seated and complete that it extends to the physiological realm, as happens in cases of hysteria. (11)

However, in keeping with Sartre's theory of emotion, we should interpret these physiological phenomena not simply as resulting from the belief that the other is "a Jew," but also contributing, even constituting, the color of that belief. To identify the other as "a Jew" and then to just say "I hate Jews" is not to hate Jews. That can only be disingenuous anti-Semitism. The physiological phenomena associated with the identification of "the Jew," however, make the hatred real, believable. In order for that designation of an object as, say, disgusting to ring true, one must feel disgust in the presence of the object.

Another point made by Sartre in relation to physiological phenomena associated with anti-Semitism is that statements of the type "There must be *something* about the Jews; they upset me physically" derive from "the logic of passion" (10). This can be connected to what has been said earlier about the relation between emotion and passion in Sartre's thought. In this case, the anti-Semite's claim that, in effect, his hatred of "the Jew" is a matter of passion, is a claim that his hatred is imposed on him from the outside, it is something he suffers. But this can only serve to underscore his bad faith. His *passion* is in fact *emotion*, an act of consciousness; not something caused by the world, but rather an attitude toward the world from within. The anti-Semite makes the Jew disgusting by experiencing disgust in the presence of the Jew.

This "making the Jew disgusting" can also be understood through reference to Sartre's ideas about intentionality and the role played by consciousness in constituting its object. We saw in chapter 1 that while Sartre is not an idealist (he thinks that there really is a world out there) he still holds that consciousness plays a constitutive role with respect to its objects. Especially in Sartre's account of emotion, we see consciousness coloring its objects.

The importance of Sartre's theory of emotion for us here is that, as limited as it may be, it does provide an explanation of how it can arise that a person holds irrational beliefs as part of a strategy to avoid difficulties in the world. By accounting for irrational beliefs in this way, the holding of those beliefs can be seen as being involved in a wider project of self-situation in the world. Rather than this process being a matter of shaping the self in light of experiences in the perceived world, we can see it as a dialectic in which both the self and the world are shaped. However, in a Sartrean framework, perception of the world is always linked to some project of self-formation. The world appears to us in relation to our projects and our projects constitute our self-formation. What makes the anti-Semite's style of self-formation different from that which Sartre would recommend? The answer to this lies in Sartre's definition of authenticity in *Anti-Semite and Jew*. "Authenticity . . . consists in having a true and lucid consciousness of the situation, in assuming the responsibilities and risks that it involves" (90). What is characteristic of the anti-Semite's response to his situation is that he precisely does not have "a true and lucid consciousness of the situation," but rather develops a view of his situation that clouds over the difficulties that it harbors. His response is to adopt Manichaeism, a simplistic, irresponsible, and extremist worldview that refuses to examine the complexities of his true situation.

Sartre's theory of emotion is also important to understanding not simply how irrationality might be conducted, but also how the anti-Semite's irrationality is lived. In emotion, consciousness can give its objects qualities of hatefulness and repellence. The anti-Semite's beliefs about "the Jew" are not simply mistaken. It is not that the anti-Semite has certain data at his disposal that he somehow jumbles up or misunderstands. The anti-Semite *makes* "the Jew" an evil, hateful object in his (the anti-Semite's) world. However, this does not mean that we should interpret the anti-Semite as a victim of a particular interpretation of the world. As we also saw in chapter 1, consciousness is always nonpositionally aware of itself. This includes emotional consciousness.

Also, it is always possible to reflect on one's emotion and see it for what it is: a conscious act directed at the world, not something forced on one by the world.

There remains one aspect of anti-Semitism that has not yet been discussed. If the role of "the Jew" is as object of the anti-Semite's passion, what is the role of actual Jewish people? On Sartre's account, anti-Semitism appears as something stemming not from the nature of Jewish people, but from the anti-Semite's refusal of freedom, for himself and for others. The Manichaean worldview requires that someone play the role of the enemy. In anti-Semitism "the Jew" is constructed to play this role. But why are actual Jewish people selected to fulfill the role of this stereotype? A different kind of study is called for at this point, one that would make reference to historical and cultural factors. We can imagine some outlines and structures of possible explanations. Given the anti-Semite's fascination with tradition, for example, he might be pleased simply to adopt the traditional anti-Semitism of his forebears. Alternatively, the anti-Semite, though lacking the pedigree of the "traditional" anti-Semite, might still make use of the ready-made focus of hatred that traditional anti-Semitism provides to defuse his frustrations. The results of the study might prove to be applicable also to other sorts of racism, like the hatred of "Blacks" or "Asians" that occurs in different societies and cultures.[37] But the important point for the structure of the Sartrean account is that once the emotional response has been engaged, and Manichaeism is set in place, someone must play the role of villain. As Sartre says: "If the Jew did not exist, the anti-Semite would invent him."[38]

Thus the role played by actual Jewish people in Sartre's account of anti-Semitism emerges as marginal, almost incidental. Jewish people are the victims of anti-Semitism not its cause. It is not even through a misapprehension of Jewish people that anti-Semitism is entered into. Anti-Semitism is a response to the anti-Semite's own situation. Actual people play little if any role in this situation, yet they are the victims of the response to it. As Sartre writes, the anti-Semite "is a man who is afraid. Not of the Jews, . . . but of himself, of his own consciousness, of his liberty, of his instincts, of his responsibilities, of solitariness, of change, of society, and of the world—of everything except the Jews"

(53). Given the devastating consequences on the Jewish people that history has shown anti-Semitism to have, and the persistence of anti-Semitism in many societies today, this is indeed a chilling realization.

Anti-Semitism and racism in general are complex phenomena, admitting various interpretations and explanations depending on the particular situation at hand, such that no single paradigmatic account is possible. In fact some theorists refer to "racisms," rather than "racism," in order to underscore the multifarious nature of racist manifestations.[39] Elements such as ideology, power, or irrationality may be at work, individually or in concert, in a case of racism.[40] I believe that Sartre's account, while not exhaustive, can be useful in understanding certain racist scenarios. It can be so particularly in cases where irrational belief plays a central role. Rather than simply attributing racist irrationality to cognitive deficiency or sloppy thinking, Sartre provides, through the notion of bad faith, an account of what might motivate an engagement in such irrationality. This, furthermore, invites us to maintain a focus on racists as responsible (or irresponsible) agents who can and should be held accountable for their acts.

NOTES

1. I am assuming that anti-Semitism is an example of racism, and that at least some of the results of an analysis of anti-Semitism will be applicable to racism in general. A recent contribution to the study of racism from a Sartrean perspective is Lewis Gordon, *Bad Faith and Anti-Black Racism*. As the title suggests, Gordon concentrates specifically on racism targeted at "Blacks." He interprets this racism in terms of bad faith and presents an excellent existential phenomenological analysis of being black in an anti-black world. Apart from the fact that it does not concentrate on anti-black racism, my analysis differs from Gordon's by focusing on the dual nature of bad faith (something that receives less explicit attention in Gordon's work) and by applying it to oppression in a wider sense.

2. Sartre is clearly referring to just one of the ways in which the term *opinion* can be used. There are other ways of employing this term. For example, when we go to a doctor to seek her "medical opinion" on some matter, we are not after an expression of her tastes. Rather, in this case *opinion* refers to an educated and considered judgment.

3. Sartre, *Anti-Semite and Jew*, 7–8.

4. The character that Sartre calls "the anti-Semite" in *Anti-Semite and Jew* is male, and I will employ the male pronoun when speaking of Sartre's character.

5. Sartre, *Anti-Semite and Jew*, 8.

6. A similar point, made in relation to racist hate speech, can be found in J. L. A. Garcia, "The Heart of Racism," 16.

7. Sartre, *Anti-Semite and Jew*, 10.

8. The term *Manichaeism*, which Sartre uses metaphorically in *Anti-Semite and Jew*, alludes to the religion of the same name. Manichaeism was a Persian religion of late antiquity that adhered to "a consistent dualism which rejects any possibility of tracing the origins of good and evil to one and the same source. . . . The present world, and man in particular, presents a mixture Good and Evil, [which is] the result of a breach of the original limits by the powers of evil. The whole purpose of the founding of the universe was to separate the two principles and restore the original state of affairs, rendering Evil forever harmless and preventing any future repetition of the intermingling" (R. McL. Wilson, "Mani and Manichaeism," 149).

9. Sartre, *Anti-Semite and Jew*, 40–41.

10. I employ quotes to indicate that "the Jew" is a caricature of real Jews, constructed by the anti-Semite to fill a niche in his Manichaean world, and I am forced to do so quite often. I trust that the reader will appreciate the importance of distinguishing "the Jew" (as the anti-Semite conceives her) from actual Jewish people. In using this notation, I in no way intend to diminish the tragic impact that the notion of "the Jew" can have on actual Jewish people.

11. Sartre, *Anti-Semite and Jew*, 34.

12. *Passion*, for Sartre, is the experience of emotion as something forced upon the subject by the object of the emotion, which, as we shall see, is deemed by Sartre to be an erroneous interpretation of emotion. The passion/emotion distinction will receive more attention in the next section of this chapter.

13. William James, *The Principles of Psychology*, 743.

14. Sartre, *The Emotions*, 22.

15. Gregory McCulloch, *Using Sartre*, 18–19.

16. Sartre, *The Emotions*, 58.

17. Hazel E. Barnes, "Sartre on the Emotions," 73–74.

18. Sartre, *The Emotions*, 26. It should be noted that I have replaced "physiological," which appears in Frechtman's translation, with "psychological," thereby correcting a mistranslation.

19. Actually, Sartre claims that Janet does implicitly presuppose finality, but that his theory explicitly rejects it.

20. Note that the phrase "the state alone would not provoke the demeanor" connects with Sartre's criticism (discussed earlier) of James's theory of emotion, which, according to Sartre, focuses only on physiological phenomena and ignores the demeanors that characterize different emotions.

21. Joseph P. Fell, *Emotion in the Thought of Sartre*, chapter 8. There are many more criticisms that could be leveled at Sartre's theory than those that I am addressing. Apart from Fell's book and the articles by Barnes and Weberman that I refer to in this chapter, one finds useful lines of criticism in Robert Solomon, "Sartre on Emotions."

22. Sartre's claim that emotional behavior is uninstrumental should not be taken to imply that emotional behavior is therefore not aimed at some goal. For Sartre, emotional behavior most certainly is goal-directed. The point Sartre wants to make is that in pursuing its goal, emotional behavior is not carried out in accordance with the rules of instrumentality.

23. Sartre, *The Emotions*, 80. Emphasis mine.

24. Fell, *Emotion in the Thought of Sartre*, 135.

25. Sartre, *The Emotions*, 60.

26. Presumably "calculation" can refer simply to an observed aspect of behavior, namely that the behavior operates in accordance with the rules of instrumentality and does not require that the subject in question operate reflectively in the light of those rules.

27. Fell, *Emotion in the Thought of Sartre*, 135.

28. Sartre, *The Emotions*, 69.

29. David Weberman also criticizes Sartre's theory of emotion with respect to its capacity to cover positive emotions. Weberman denies that most positive emotions involve the "immense expectations" that Sartre attributes them, such that they, in fact, do not require "magical incantations" (Weberman, "Sartre, Emotions, and Wallowing," 397).

30. Fell, *Emotion in the Thought of Sartre*, 120–21.

31. Sartre, *Anti-Semite and Jew*, 54.

32. "For the anti-Semite, what makes the Jew is the presence in him of 'Jewishness,' a Jewish principle analogous to phlogiston or the soporific virtue of opium" (Sartre, *Anti-Semite and Jew*, 37).

33. Sartre, "The Childhood of a Leader," 186.

34. Sartre, *Anti-Semite and Jew*, 18–19.

35. Of course, sometimes one's race *is* a (probably, though not necessarily, illegitimate) determining factor, and a clear and lucid appraisal of the situation would have to include it as such. However, the assumption here is that in the two cases cited, the inclusion of race as a contributing factor is misplaced.

36. Sartre, *Anti-Semite and Jew*, 10.

37. In saying this I do not mean to suggest that all instances of racism will be best described in these terms. I do not even believe that all instances of anti-Semitism will admit such an explanation. But the maneuver discussed here, whereby the racist transforms the world to live in the particular form of bad faith that Sartre attributes to the anti-Semite, could sometimes prove to be present in other forms of racism.

38. Sartre, *Anti-Semite and Jew*, 13.

39. For examples see Kwame Anthony Appiah, "Racisms," 3–17, and David Theo Goldberg, "Racist Exclusions."

40. Goldberg, "Racist Exclusions," 1–5.

4

Others in the World of the Self

In the last chapter I examined Sartre's account of anti-Semitism in terms of bad faith. Through this examination racism emerged as involving a refusal of ambiguity, a refusal to embrace the human condition of being a freedom in situation. Anti-Semitism, as with the other cases of bad faith examined thus far, involves others: other anti-Semites, Jews, restaurant patrons, and so on. However, to this point I have focused on anti-Semitism and bad faith insofar as they are individual endeavors to modify the human condition, with others figuring simply as possible objects of consciousness. But others are not simply objects; they are human subjects, and the effect that they can have on the for-itself, as competing consciousnesses, plays a vital role in the motivation for and practice of oppression. Oppression is oppression of someone, another human subject or collectivity of subjects, and understanding the way in which an oppressor deals with the subjectivity of those others, and how those others may affect the subjectivity of the oppressor, is vital to any understanding of oppression.

It is the aim of this chapter to examine Sartre's account of the ontological bases, structures, and dynamics of intersubjectivity. First, I will examine *being-for-others*, the aspect of the being of the for-itself that emerges when the for-itself experiences itself being experienced, from the outside, by an other. As we shall see, being-for-others constitutes a significant part of the facticity of being-for-itself. Second, it will be necessary to consider what Sartre takes to be the fundamental project of being-for-itself: the desire to become a being-in-itself-for-itself, that is, to become "God." This will be a necessary prelude to an examination of Sartre's analysis of concrete relations with others, on the level of one-to-one intersubjectivity and on the level of sociality. This is an important topic to examine, as relations with others (even though they may take an unethical form) are central to oppression. We will see that the relations with others described by Sartre are engaged in an attempt to realize the goal of becoming "God" and are conducted in bad faith. Finally, having developed an account of relations with others I will reexamine the case of the anti-Semite from chapter 3, this time framing it in terms of collective activity in relation to others.

BEING-FOR-OTHERS

In chapter 1 I examined the two fundamental modes of being that appear in Sartre's ontology: being-for-itself and being-in-itself. There we saw being-for-itself as conscious being and being-in-itself as the being of objects, where *object* is construed as referring to anything under the governance of the principle of identity. There exists also a third mode of being that holds an important place in the ontology, and that mode is being-for-others. Being-for-others is a mode of being in which the for-itself exists as an object for another consciousness.

In *Being and Nothingness*, Sartre provides the following example to illustrate being-for-others. There is a man who, through jealousy or curiosity, is looking through a keyhole. He is "alone and on the level of non-thetic self-consciousness,"[1] which is to say that he is prereflectively conscious of his objects and does not inhabit his consciousness as a self that is acting in a certain way. He focuses only on the world that lies on the other side of the door. All that he is aware of is the keyhole and the scene that he sees through it. Suddenly he hears footsteps behind him in the hallway. Immediately he becomes conscious of himself as he may appear to others: a man, on his knees, spying on someone or something through the keyhole of a door. He is aware of the presence of a voyeur. He is aware of himself. Just as the people on the other side of the door were objects in his world, he is now an object in the world of an other (259–60).

Being-for-others is basically a species of being-in-itself, though a rather special one. What makes being-for-others a species of being-in-itself is its character as an objectification. Sartre writes, "I grasp the Other's look at the very center of my act as the solidification and alienation of my own possibilities" (263). In the example in the preceding paragraph, the voyeur, upon hearing the creak in the floorboards and inferring that he is in the presence of an other, experiences himself as an object in the world of an other. He sees himself fixed in the present with the qualities that he imagines his observer perceives him to have. In his being-for-others, he simply is what he is. It is the applicability of the principle of identity to being-for-others that reveals its nature as a species of being-in-itself. "Shame [a fundamental experience of being-for-others] reveals to me that I *am* this being, not in the mode of 'was' or of 'having to be' but *in-itself*" (262). Elsewhere Sartre describes being-for-others as "this unjustifiable being-in-itself which I am for the Other" (222). Simple objects such as tables and chairs do not have being-for-others, even though their being-in-itself is in part constituted by consciousness. Only beings-for-themselves have being-for-others. Being-for-others emerges only through intersubjectivity.[2]

The type of object generated through being-for-others is quite different from "this pen" or "the house on the hill." The following example from *Being and Nothingness* illustrates this. Imagine that I am standing in a park. I look around and see a lawn bisected by a path. On the far side of the path there is a fountain, bubbling away, and there are benches dotted along the length of the path. All of these things are objects in my world. I can speak of the relations between these objects. This bench is eight meters away from that bench. The fountain is six meters away from the first bench, ten meters from the second, and so on. The important thing to realize here is that, whatever the relations are between the things in this world, I am at its center. I give it meaning. I am the referential center for the array of meaningful objects in the world. Now imagine that I see a man standing by the fountain. Is he simply another object among all of the others in my world? If this were so

> his relation with other objects would be of a purely additive type; this means that I could have him disappear without the relations of the other objects around him being perceptibly changed. In short, no new relation would appear *through him* between those things in my universe: grouped and synthesized *from my point of view.*[3]

But by perceiving him to be a man, I am in fact forced to perceive the world differently. I cannot *simply* perceive that he is one meter away from the fountain (although that may be true) in the same way that I perceive the fountain to be six meters away from the bench. This is because by perceiving him to be a man, I perceive that things are ordered or arranged around him as they were ordered around me. Sartre writes that here "we are dealing with a relation . . . inside of which there unfolds a spatiality which is not *my* spatiality; for instead of a grouping *toward me* of the objects, there is now an orientation *which flees from me*" (254). If, however, I were to realize that I was mistaken (for example, it is not really a man after all, merely a statue) I would revert to my position as referential center of the world, and his (the statue's) relationship with the other objects *would* be of a purely additive type.

However, let us stay with the situation in which I perceive him to be a man. Despite the fact that he cannot be simply added to the other objects in my field, like another bench or tree, he is still for me an object (the object posited by my consciousness), albeit an object of a special type. Although all objects have aspects that one is unable to perceive at any given time (an object can be perceived from an infinite number of perspectives but, clearly, not from all of them simultaneously) the hidden aspects of the man-object are of an altogether different order. Take for example the hidden aspects of one of the benches. These would include its appearance from different distances and angles, its weight, its texture, and so on. While these aspects may elude me while I stand at a fixed point in space just looking at it, I could in principle perceive any of these by simply changing my position. I could walk around it, observing it from different points. I could walk up to it and run my hand over its surface in order to feel its texture. I could try lifting it to see how heavy it is. However, in the case of the man there are hidden aspects that will always remain so. I could, of course, find out what he looks like from different angles, try to lift him to see how much he weighs, and so on. But there are hidden aspects of him to which I will always be denied access. These are to do with the world as it appears to him: not the physical aspects of it but its meanings. He gives meanings to the things in his world and these will differ from those that I have given to mine, at the very least by the mere fact that it is *he* rather than *I* that is their source.

However, the object that we have described thus far is the object that emerges from the objectification of a for-itself by an other seen from the perspective of the other. It is, if you like, the other side of being-for-others, that is, the other's experience of what occurs in the objectification of a person. Being-for-others, however, is the experience of this objectification from the point of view of the one objectified. Let us return to the park. At this stage the man is unaware of my presence. Now imagine that he turns around and looks at me. Now I am an object for him, as he was for me. He is no longer the other-as-object, but the other-as-subject. Prior to this I noticed that he was in control of the meanings of the objects in his world. Now I too am one of those objects, and, at my realization of this, my mode of being changes. I no longer have being-for-myself, but being-for-others.

Sartre tends to cast being-for-others in a negative light. For example, through my being-for-others I am stripped of my transcendence (262); the experience of the other's look marks "the death of my possibilities" (264); as an object for an other I am "degraded" (273). Sartre presents being-for-others primarily as a threat to the for-itself's subjectivity, a threat of enslavement by the freedom of the other. However I must take issue with Sartre on this point. Being-for-others need not always be understood in terms of threat and degradation. If the other interprets the self positively, the self may experience pride, rather than shame, upon the realization of its being-for-others.[4] Examples of this might include an actor who receives a standing ovation for her performance, or a man who realizes that someone has witnessed him behaving admirably. Being the object of the caring look of a loved one can be a source of comfort and security rather than alienation and degradation. Apart from this, being-for-others does grant the self some substance. Part of the for-itself's anguish is caused by its unfoundedness, its floating and indeterminate nature. With being-for-others, the self can see itself, through the eyes of others, as really being there and really being something.

However, Sartre spends little time exploring the possible positive aspects of being-for-others, concentrating instead on the negative aspects. As being-for-others results from the other's free interpretation of the self, the self has little control over this aspect of its being. Certainly, it can attempt to project a certain image in the hope that its being-for-others will turn out the way that it would like, but it can never really be sure of achieving this. The other's status as a freely interpreting being, which is the basis of being-for-others, makes being-for-others a risky and uncertain state.

Sartre's rather bleak approach to being-for-others can be interpreted as an example of his tendency, at times, to overemphasize the role of transcendence, to the exclusion of facticity, in human being; that is, to neglect the situatedness of freedom. In chapter 1 we saw that sometimes Sartre portrays human reality as unbridled freedom, transcending all facticity. Following this way of thinking about human being, the idea of another person holding the key to an aspect of one's being stands as an affront to one's subjectivity. The other's interpretation of the for-itself is beyond the for-itself's control, leaving the for-itself at the mercy of the other. Also, being-for-others, as a form of facticity, places limits on the freedom of the for-itself. Both of these aspects of being-for-others would appear to Sartre, in his moments of more extreme libertarianism, as degradations of the transcendent subject. However, I also claimed in chapter 1 that another interpretation of human reality could be found in *Being and Nothingness*, one that accepts the important role of facticity to human being through situating freedom. When greater emphasis is placed on the role of facticity, the possibly positive, constructive role that being-for-others might play in the life of the for-itself becomes more apparent.

However, having said this, being-for-others will often be a negative, conflictual experience. The look of the other can be hostile, even if it does not always have to be so. This can surely be an alienating experience. Sartre presents encounters with others, and the being-for-others emerging from such encounters, as challenges to the freedom and subjectivity of the for-itself, challenges that must be met with either struggle against or surrender to the freedom of the other. We will discuss further the conflictual aspects of being-for-others in the section on concrete relations with others.

Although being-for-others is the experience of a for-itself existing as an object in the world of an other, a for-itself can have being-for-others even if there is no other actually there. In the example of the voyeur, even if the supposed presence of the other were merely a creak in the floorboards, the voyeur could still experience himself as being-for-others. But one can go further still, and say that a person need not even be aware, mistakenly or not, of the presence of an other. Having experienced itself as being-for-others, a for-itself can from then on adopt, to a degree at least, the role of other to itself, that is, can reflect upon itself from the point of view of an imaginary other.[5] In other words, being-for-others should not be seen as a time-to-time, chance occurrence intruding on the otherwise insular being-for-itself, but rather as an ever-present mode of being in the life of an individual:

> Upon any one of my conducts it is *always* possible to converge two looks, mine and that of the Other. The conduct will not present exactly the same structure in each case. . . . As each look perceives it, there is between these two aspects of my being, no difference between appearance and being—as if I were to my self the truth of myself and as if the Other possessed only a deformed image of me. The equal dignity of being, possessed by my being-for-others and my being-for-myself permits a perpetually disintegrating synthesis and a perpetual game of escape from the for-itself to the for-others and from the for-others to the for-itself.[6]

Thus, being-for-others stands as a crucial and ever-present aspect of human reality.

RELATIONS WITH OTHERS

The condition of intersubjectivity, as presented by Sartre in *Being and Nothingness*, can both propel the for-itself into, and be read in terms of, what we might call the *God project*. As we have seen in chapter 1, being-for-itself lacks identity with itself. However, this lack is something that being-for-itself strives to fill. Being-for-itself desires the solid, self-identity of being-in-itself. But being-for-itself also desires to escape contingency, and thereby seeks to found its own being. The goal of this desire, which is being-for-itself's fundamental existential project, is a synthesis of the two regions of being, which is to say that being-for-itself desires to become a being-in-itself-for-itself. As such

> each human reality is at the same time a direct project to metamorphose its own For-itself into an In-itself-For-itself and a project of the appropriation of the world as a totality of being-in-itself, in the form of a fundamental quality. Every human reality is a passion in that it projects losing itself so as to found being and by the same stroke to constitute the In-itself which escapes contingency by being its own foundation, the *Ens causa sui*, which religions call God. Thus the passion of man is the reverse of that of Christ, for man loses himself as man in order that God may be born. But the idea of God is contradictory and we lose ourselves in vain. Man is a useless passion. (615)

"God" as being-in-itself-for-itself is impossible because such a synthesis of the two regions of being would produce a contradiction. To the extent that a being is self-identical (being-in-itself), it cannot be free (being-for-itself), as non-self-identity and lack of substantial being is a condition of freedom. Similarly, to the extent that such a being is for-itself, and thereby free and lacking in self-identity, it cannot have the solid being of an in-itself. Thus the goal of human reality's fundamental project is an impossible one.[7] Furthermore, the God project aims at "solving" the ambiguity of human reality, and so stands as a project pursued in bad faith.

We have seen that being-for-others is an objectification of being-for-itself by an other and that being-for-others is experienced as being conferred from the outside. As the result of this conferral by the free consciousness of the other, being-for-others is beyond the control of the self. Sartre holds that in experiencing being-for-others, the self is confronted by an objective mode of its own being, and must react to this in some way. Given the God project, intersubjectivity propels the self into an attempt to achieve a synthesis of its being-for-itself and its being-for-others.

In the section of *Being and Nothingness* entitled "Concrete Relations with Others," Sartre explores the possibilities of intersubjectivity when subsumed under, or conducted in the light of, the God project. His analysis considers a variety of relations with others involving different strategies that a for-itself may employ in attempting to deal with its being-for-others. It is here that we see the one-who-looks/one-who-is-looked-at dichotomy at work in various combinations. The importance of these various kinds of relations with others to understanding oppression is threefold. First, each contains elements of bad faith that have been discussed in earlier chapters, but does so specifically in the context of relations with others. As oppression involves relations with others, we need to understand what form such relations may take. Second, if Sartre's early philosophy is useful for the purpose of interpreting at least some cases of oppression (an intersubjective phenomenon), we might expect to witness in those cases one or more of the kinds of intersubjective arrangements that emerge from his work. In chapter 5, I will examine an example of sexism in which one such arrangement is manifest. Finally, the account of concrete relations with others leads us also to Sartre's account of collective activity, which is important if we are to understand the collective/social dimension of oppression.

Relations with an Other

The presence of an other confers being-for-others, a species of being-in-itself, upon the self. Given the self's desire to become an in-itself-for-itself, that is, an in-itself that is its own foundation (which is a desire to escape ambiguity), the self both wants to be its being-for-others and to not be its being-for-others. The self desires to be the object it is for the other, as that part of the God project that aims at the in-itself. Yet the self also desires not to be the object it is for the other, because the other part of the God project is to attain for the self the status of free foundation of itself, and it is precisely *the other* who is the foundation of the self's being-for-others. "Thus," Sartre claims, "the for-itself is both a flight and a pursuit; it flees the in-itself and at the same time pursues it."[8] However, these two desires are clearly opposed. As we have seen, the synthesis of the in-itself and the for-itself, which is the aim of the God project, is impossible. The self cannot pursue both desires simultaneously.[9] Hence, when faced with the situation of being an object for an other, the self can *either* pursue it *or* flee it.

The first attitude that may be taken with respect to the object one is for the other is to pursue it. To the extent that the for-itself seeks substantial being, the being there and being something that the other's evaluation provides can tantalize the for-itself. Of this attitude Sartre writes:

> In so far as the Other as freedom is the foundation of my being-in-itself, I can seek to recover that freedom and to possess it without removing from it its character as freedom. In fact if I could identify myself with that freedom which is the foundation of my being-in-itself, I should be to myself my own foundation.[10]

Rather than deny the object that it is for the other, the for-itself accepts the other's evaluation and attempts to identify itself with the other's freedom, which has produced it. Sartre describes love and masochism as pursuits conducted along the lines of this strategy. In love, the for-itself attempts to appropriate the freedom of the other, the freedom that has conferred upon the for-itself its being as object-for-the-other (366–77). In masochism the for-itself's project is to become absorbed by the other's subjectivity such that the for-itself's subjectivity is lost entirely (378–79). However, the strategies of possession or capture of the other's freedom on the one hand, and absorption by the other's freedom on the other, are doomed to failure. To the extent that the for-itself can grasp or have some purchase on the other's freedom, the other's freedom ceases to be freedom. To the extent that the other's freedom remains as freedom, it is wholly the other's. Furthermore, as this strategy involves the self wholly identifying with itself as object for the other, it stands as an example of that type of bad faith in which one denies one's freedom in order to identify oneself with facticity.

The second attitude one can take toward the object that one is for the other is to flee or deny it. Sartre explains that when the Other *looks* at me . . . he holds the secret of my being, he knows what I am. Thus the profound meaning of my being is outside of me, imprisoned in an absence. The Other has the advantage over me. Therefore in so far as I am fleeing the in-itself which I am without founding it, I can attempt to deny that being which is conferred on me from outside; that is, I can turn back upon the Other so as to make an object out of him in turn since the Other's object-ness destroys my object-ness for him. (363)

By looking back at the other, by objectifying the other, by freezing the other's possibilities through the look and rendering the other as object, the for-itself can flee its being-for-others. One has being-for-others conferred on one by another subject. Turn the other into an object and being-for-others can be escaped. This, at least, is the rationale behind the strategy that founds the relations with others designated by Sartre as indifference, desire, sadism, and hate. Indifference involves blindness toward others, an ignoring of their subjectivity (380–82). In desire and sadism the for-itself attempts to ensnare the other's freedom in the other's being-as-object either through the caressing of the other's body (in the case of desire) (382–98) or the infliction of pain on the other's body (in the case of sadism) (399–406). Finally, in hate the for-itself attempts to escape its being-for-others by pursuing the death of the other, or at least "projecting the realization of a world in which the Other does not exist" (410–12).

However, these strategies cannot be successful either. While it is true that a simple object cannot confer being-for-others on the self, the other, even objectified, is not such a simple object. The other is initially recognized as a subject; after all, it is the experience of the other's look that motivates the looking back. This recognition of the other's subjectivity haunts the project of rendering the other a permanent object, and hence this project can only be conducted in bad faith. It is only by self-deceptively ignoring the other's subjectivity that such a project can hope to succeed, and such hopes are grounded in bad faith. Even in indifference and hate, where the other is ignored or even wished away entirely, the for-itself will find no escape from its being-for-others. This is because "he who has once been for-others is contaminated in his being for the rest of his days even if the Other should be entirely suppressed; he will never cease to apprehend his dimension of being-for-others as a permanent possibility of his being" (412). The world of others is inescapable.

Neither of the two general strategies for dealing with one's being an object for an other can be successful and, furthermore, they are opposed to one another. "Each attempt is the death of the other; that is, the failure of the one motivates the adoption of the other. Thus there is no dialectic for my relations toward the Other but rather a circle— although each attempt is enriched by the failure of the other" (363). The series of relations with the other that Sartre presents gives a bleak picture of intersubjectivity. All of these relations are impossible to maintain and can never achieve the goals they set for themselves. What is more, the failure of one relation can only motivate the adoption of another member of this dire circle. Sartre writes early in the section on concrete relations with others that "conflict is the original meaning of being-for-others" (364), and he remains true to his word throughout his analysis. All concrete relations with the other are fraught with conflict and haunted by their inevitable failure.

However there does appear in *Being and Nothingness* a footnote suggesting that perhaps this is not all that could be expected of inter-subjectivity. In it Sartre writes: "These considerations [on concrete relations with others] do not exclude the possibility of an ethics of deliverance and salvation. But this can be achieved only after a radical conversion which we can not discuss here" (412). While a fuller analysis of this "radical conversion" will not be conducted here either,[11] a sketch of what Sartre means by this can be given. If the possibilities for intersubjectivity that Sartre provides appear inauthentic, that is because they are just that. They all involve various forms of bad faith and they do so at different levels. First, each individual relation has its own characteristic configuration or combination of bad faith maneuvers. For example, masochism involves bad faith beliefs about oneself (that one could wholly identify oneself with one's being-an-object-for-the-other) and the other (that the other is pure subjectivity), while indifference involves one ignoring in bad faith one's being-in-the-midst-of-the-world and ignoring the subjectivity of others and their ability to see one in one's facticity. Second, the concrete relations with others that Sartre describes in *Being and Nothingness* are all conducted within the God project, which, as we have seen, is itself a project conducted in bad faith. The goal of the God project is an impossible one, the impossibility of which is ignored in bad faith by the pursuer of the project. In other words, all of these relations with others are pursued in bad faith.[12] In fact, bad faith is necessary to each of them. If we take these relations as involving bad faith they can provide insight into how oppression operates, rather than being characteristic of all that is possible in intersubjectivity in general. The radical conversion that Sartre alludes to is a conversion from the God project and bad faith to authenticity. It involves an acceptance of the ambiguity of human reality both for oneself and for others and an embracing of freedom as situated. The result of this conversion would be that the other does not necessarily pose a threat to the self, the only possible responses to which are retaliation or submission. In other words, the conversion would lead one out of the circle of relations with others described by Sartre.

Collective Intersubjectivity: The Us-Object and We-Subject

To this point the discussion of relations between the for-itself and others has focused on scenarios in which there is a single other. But relations with others also imply a wider social dimension. What happens when more than two people are involved? Sartre discusses two further categories of being, the *we-subject* and the *us-object*, which "correspond exactly to the being-in-the-act-of-looking and the being-looked-at which constitute the fundamental relations of the For-itself and the Other."[13] While these two collective forms of being may share some of the characteristics of being on the one-to-one level (for example, taking up one or other position in a subject/object dynamic) they should not be seen as simply plural forms of their counterparts on the one-to-one level. The us-object is not simply a collection of individual beings-as-objects, nor is the we-subject simply a collection of beings-as-subjects. Rather, they are object or subject as a group.

Analysis of collective identity and relations with others is crucial to an understanding of kinds of oppression such as racism and sexism. These kinds of oppression trade on categories like race and gender, categories with group connotations. They are movements occurring on a social level and cannot be appreciated in the absence of reference to collective identities and activities. In what follows, I will examine the two main categories of collective intersubjectivity discussed in *Being and Nothingness*: the us-object and the we-subject. The introduction of the notions of the us-object and we-subject will allow us to shift the analysis of oppression from the individual to the collective. The us-object/we-subject arrangement is commensurate with the earlier analysis of the two types of bad faith; the us-object standing as a possible case of the for-itself identifying itself with its facticity, while the we-subject can involve a denial of facticity. This allows the analysis of oppression at the collective level to be mapped onto the earlier analysis of the two types of bad faith. Following the discussion of the us-object and we-subject, I will frame the earlier analysis of anti-Semitism in terms of the operations of an us-object. In the next chapter, a mode of oppression analyzable in terms of the operations of a we-subject will be examined. Let us turn first to the us-object.

The us-object arises when the for-itself and an other (or others) fall under the gaze of a third party. When this happens, "I experience the existence of an objective situation-form in the world of the Third in which the Other and I shall figure as *equivalent* structures in *solidarity* with each other" (418). In such a situation, whatever conflict the for-itself and the other may have been engaged in is transcended by the third. The for-itself, the other, and their relations with each other become a part of the world of the third, in which they exist as an objective totality. "Thus what I experience is a being-outside in which I am organized with the Other in an indissoluble objective whole, a whole in which I am fundamentally *no longer distinct* from the Other but which I agree in solidarity with the Other to constitute" (418). Sartre describes the us-object as "a simple enrichment of the original proof of the for-others" (429), which is to say that it is a variation of being-for-others. Instead of a single for-itself experiencing itself as the object for an other, as was described earlier as being-for-others, in the case of the us-object a for-itself experiences itself in a communion of objectivity with an other, both of whom fall under the gaze of a third. I will deal with the us-object in more detail later in this chapter.

In the we-subject, a for-itself experiences itself as a member of a "subject-community" (423), whose look is directed at a (shared) object. Being part of the audience at the cinema could stand as an example of the we-subject. I am there as a subject, an observer, and evaluator of the images on the screen. But I am not alone in this project. I am surrounded by others who are also watching and evaluating the film and, given our shared object, there is some sense of community that arises among us. However, Sartre claims that the sense of community generated by the we-subject is quite illusory. While Sartre holds that the us-object is an experience of the ontological order (as an enrichment of being-for-others), the we-subject is purely "psychological . . . [and] in no way corresponds to a real unification of the for-itselfs under consideration" (424). The us-object is a real, though unstable, part of the ontological landscape of sociality.[14] The "them" exists in the world as an object for a third. However, the we-subject does not share this property of actual collectivity. "Thus," Sartre writes, "there is no symmetry between the making proof of the Us-object and the experience of the We-subject."[15]

Why is it that Sartre designates the we-subject as somehow less important than the us-object?[16] This is an important question to raise because in the next chapter I will argue that there are examples of oppression that can be understood as arising from the activity of an oppressive we-subject. If the ontological status of the we-subject were questionable, this would surely cast doubt on the viability of an analysis that employed the we-subject as one of its primary terms. Sartre can accept the ontological status of the self-as-subject and the self-as-object-for-an-other in one-to-one relations. Yet on the collective level he can accept only the ontological status of the us-object (which at the collective level parallels the self-as-object-for-an-other). Why must the we-subject be understood as psychological and not ontological? I will argue later that by realizing that facticity must still be taken into account when discussing the we-subject, despite the we-subject's attempted ignoring of facticity, the concept of the we-subject can be attributed more significant ontological status. However, before doing this, let us examine possible reasons for holding that the we-subject is purely psychological.

One possibility is that any recognition of the we-subject by one of its members can only be a non-thetic awareness of the others that are taken to be a part of it. These others cannot be posited by the for-itself, for if they were posited they would cease to appear as subjects in alignment with the for-itself, and would instead be objects for the for-itself. This is strongly reminiscent of Sartre's treatment of pre-reflective consciousness. It will be recalled from chapter 1 that in pre-reflective consciousness there is an object posited by consciousness and that this positional consciousness is accompanied by a non-positional awareness of itself as consciousness. In the case of the we-subject there is an object posited jointly by the subjectivities that make up the we-subject, and the we-subjectness of the positing is recognized by the for-itself (which takes itself to be a part of the we) through a non-positional awareness of the others engaged in the positing. It will also be recalled that in reflective consciousness, where the for-itself posits itself as the object, it misses itself as there is no simple identity between the self-positing and the self-posited. Similarly, in the case of the we-subject, any positional awareness of the we-subject by the for-itself will necessarily miss the mark as the object posited is by necessity not the subject positing. But this "missing the mark" is clearly even more so in the case of the we-subject, as the positing of the we-subject is not performed by the we-subject at all, but by one of the individual for-itselves that make it up.

However, this inability of the for-itself to posit the we-subject cannot be the reason for the we-subject's lesser ontological significance, as the situation is the same in the case of the us-object. In the case of the us-object the for-itself, by positing the us-object and thereby taking up a position of subject in opposition to it would cease to be a part of the us-object. What does make the difference between the us-object and the we-subject is that while the former can be experienced directly as a part of the world (through my experience of the gaze of the third, I directly perceive the third as other-as-subject, and myself as part of an us-object), the latter can only be experienced indirectly via the object, and inferred from prior experience of others. In other words the we-subject cannot involve the direct apprehension of the subjectivities of the others that participate in it with the for-itself. The us-object involves direct apprehension of the third and so is a primary experience of others. The we-subject does not involve direct apprehension of the others in the we-subject, and so is not a primary experience of others. Sartre writes: "The 'we' includes a plurality of subjectivities which recognize one another as subjectivities. Nevertheless this recognition is not the object of an explicit thesis; what is explicitly posited is a common action or the object of a common perception."[17] It is only through inferring that the object of consciousness is also the object of other consciousnesses that the for-itself experiences itself as part of a we-subject. And the for-itself's knowledge of the subjectivity of others can only come through reference to some past experience of the "original proof of the other," that is, through having prior experience of being-for-others.

It is most certainly true, given Sartre's general ontology, that consciousnesses cannot immediately experience each other *as consciousnesses*. Although the subjectivity of the other is revealed to me through my being-for-others, this experience is of the other's consciousness *for which I am an object*. And it is also true that the for-itselves in a we-subject can only experience each other's *consciousnesses* non-positionally and via the object jointly posited. Thus to the extent that the we-subject is a collection of consciousnesses there can be no "real unification of the for-itselfs under consideration." However, Sartre's dismissal of the we-subject as "purely psychological" fails to take into account the actual condition of those that make up the we-subject. The impossibility of unification of the for-itselves in the we-subject only holds if we are dealing with disembodied consciousnesses. But of course we are not. Even if those in the we-subject take themselves to be purely transcendent, in reality they are unable to avoid their facticity. Their facticity is there for both their we-subject companions and for any outsider to observe. The presence of facticity in the we-subject means that the we-subject is not a matter of pure transcendence. But in human affairs we are never dealing with pure transcendence anyway. Furthermore, it is the presence of this "contaminating" facticity that allows for a greater degree of unification of the for-itselves in the we-subject than Sartre seems to allow.

In *Being and Nothingness* Sartre deals with the we-subject as a pure form and in doing this the importance of the we-subject as a social arrangement is diminished. Take for example Sartre's description of the bourgeoisie:

> The weakness of the oppressing class lies in the fact that although it has at its disposal precise and rigorous means for coercion, it is within itself profoundly anarchistic. The "bourgeois" is not only defined as a certain *homo œconomicus* disposing of a precise power and privilege in the heart of a society of a certain type; he is described inwardly as a consciousness which does not recognize its belonging to a class. (428)

Sartre's description of the bourgeoisie as lacking any recognition of itself as a class is a description of a pure we-subject. However, this description provides a reductio against the demand for interpreting a we-subject as a pure form. Surely the bourgeoisie is a class, despite what its members may believe, and surely it is far from weak. We might still interpret the bourgeoisie as a we-subject, but we must allow that it not be a pure form of the we-subject. By doing so we can allow for a real unification of its members. While the bourgeoisie may not reflectively identify themselves as a class, the membership of which is based on elements of facticity, its members would still make some recognition of their own qualities and those of their colleagues. Such recognition would be minimally necessary for the patterns of inclusion and exclusion characterizing any class to be manifested.

If we allow that the bourgeoisie is in part constituted through recognition of the facticity of and by those that make it up, can we still categorize it as a we-subject? We can if we accept that a we-subject is a community of subjects with a shared object, where by *subject* we mean *embodied consciousnesses in the world* rather than pure transcendence. Such a use of *subject* would be appropriate given the interpretation of human reality adopted in chapter 1, namely that human reality is best understood in terms of transcendence and facticity. The sense of *subject* that Sartre employs in his discussion of the we-subject is more in keeping with that other interpretation of human reality that is often accredited to him: namely that we are best understood as transcendent beings. An account of the we-subject that conforms to the situated freedom interpretation of human reality, however, allows that a community of subjects sharing an object may arise. This community would still fit the basic definition of *we-subject* (a subject-community), but would also include intra-group recognition of elements of the facticities of its members.

The notions of we-subject and us-object can be usefully employed in the interpretation of oppression. These concepts allow us to extend the analysis of oppression to the level of groups while retaining the concepts of human reality and bad faith that were gleaned from analyses of individuals. The we-subject and its role in oppression will be discussed further in the next chapter. Before that, though, let us examine the role played by the us-object in the life of the anti-Semite.

Having now got an idea of the us-object, reexamining the case of the anti-Semite in terms of the us-object will enrich our earlier account by adding a further level of analysis, which moves beyond understanding the anti-Semite as an isolated individual in opposition to "the Jew."

SARTRE'S ANTI-SEMITE AND THE US-OBJECT

While Sartre does not explicitly write of the anti-Semite in *Anti-Semite and Jew* in terms of the us-object, there is much material there that allows for such an interpretation.[18] Casting the anti-Semitism described by Sartre in terms of the operation of an us-object is important as this will bring the analysis of racism to the social level. Recall the examination and discussion concerning Sartre's portrait of the anti-Semite from chapter 3. There the discussion focused on the anti-Semite's relation to himself. The anti-Semite was seen to identify himself as an object, determined by an essence and affected by outside forces in a simple causal fashion. But there are other aspects of Sartre's anti-Semite that require further analysis, and this analysis is made possible by Sartre's category of the us-object. Let me first make a case for viewing the anti-Semite as participating in an us-object.

One of the characteristics of Sartre's anti-Semite is that he sees his anti-Semitism as a collective rather than individual project. Sartre tells us that the anti-Semite has no desire to pursue his project as an individual, and

> fears every kind of solitariness, that of the genius as much as that of the murderer; he is the man of the crowd. However small his stature, he takes every precaution to make it smaller, lest he stand out from the herd and find himself face to face with himself. He has made himself an anti-Semite because that is something one cannot be alone. The phrase, "I hate the Jews," is one uttered in chorus; in pronouncing it, one attaches himself to a tradition and to a community—the tradition and community of the mediocre.[19]

While anti-Semitism may involve, as would many other activities, collective projects, it is the way in which the anti-Semite experiences his membership of a group and the way in which he relates (or, rather, fails to relate) his group's activities to his own subjectivity, that directs us to his bad faith. He identifies himself as *being* a member of this group (as a table *is* a table), and defines the group totally through reference to "objective" criteria such as race and nationality (as a table is brown). As such his identification with the anti-Semite us-object appears as a flight toward facticity. But is it not the case that people do belong to us-objects, where the "us" is determined by such factors? For example, a member of a group of Asian people walking through a white-majority neighborhood may well feel the gaze of a third rendering her as part of an us-object that is defined as "a bunch of Asians." There would be nothing inauthentic about experiencing the situation in this way and, in fact, a lucid appraisal of the situation would probably demand it. However, were that person to identify herself totally with being a member of this us-object and ignore her individual subjectivity, which is also a crucial aspect of her being, she would have fallen into a type of bad faith paralleling the bad faith of Sartre's waiter: namely, that she was taking an aspect of her facticity (in this case, being a member of an us-object) as that which wholly defines her. This is what Sartre's anti-Semite appears to do.

In chapter 3, we saw that, on the individual level, the anti-Semite identified himself as *being* an anti-Semite in the way that a table *is* a table. On the collective level, we see a similar style of identification being maintained. The type of anti-Semitism that Sartre describes requires an experience of being part of a group. It is an attitude of "the true Frenchman, rooted in his province, in his country, borne along by a tradition twenty centuries old" (23). Sartre's anti-Semite identifies totally with his membership of this group, for it is through this membership that he has the right, even the duty, to hate "the Jews." The anti-Semite is a true Frenchman as a table is a table, and he bears his anti-Semitism as a table does its color and grain.

Furthermore, and again this can be related back to the example of the waiter, the anti-Semite distances himself from any personal responsibility for the actions that he, as a member of this group, performs. In the case of the waiter, the waiter simply does what he does as a waiter-automaton. The waiter experiences his waiter-like actions springing naturally or causally from his *being* a waiter, which he *is* in the mode of *being* an object. He is not responsible for those acts in the way that a free subject would be responsible for its choices. Similarly, the anti-Semite experiences his acts as arising naturally from his *being* an anti-Semite or his membership of an anti-Semite us-object. He is not the author of his acts. "I hate the Jews" is uttered in chorus, "It's just what we folk do around here." His ignoring the element of choice evident in his attending rallies, his abusive speech, and hateful acts, betrays the plane of bad faith on which he lives.

The anti-Semite, through identification with the us-object, can interpret his activities not only as objectively following from his being an anti-Semite, but as a part of a single project shared by all members of the us-object. Sartre writes, concerning the projects of those making up the us-object, that

> for the Third it is united into a *single* project common to that *they-as-object* which he embraced with his look and which even constitutes the unifying synthesis of this "Them." Therefore I must assume myself as apprehended by the Third as an integral part of the "Them." And this "Them" which is assumed by a subjectivity as its meaning-for-others becomes the "Us."[20]

The projects of those who constitute the us-object become, through the gaze of the third, a single (though, perhaps, complex) project of the group. Thus, not only does the anti-Semite see himself as immune from responsibility for his acts by virtue of those acts following causally from his nature, but he further distances himself from responsibility through interpreting his project as being the project of others as well.

This reducing of the projects of the individuals of an us-object to a project of the group as a whole plays a role in creating a kind of equality between the members of the us-object. Recall Sartre's earlier claim that the us-object is "a whole in which I am fundamentally *no longer distinct* from the Other" (418). To the extent that the anti-Semite is a part of the us-object, he is as good (or as bad) as any other of its members. Sartre mentions in several places in *Anti-Semite and*

Jew the importance placed on this equality by the anti-Semite. Some examples are:

> True Frenchmen, good Frenchmen are all equal, for each of them possesses for himself alone France whole and indivisible.[21]

> It is in protest *against* the hierarchy of functions that the anti-Semite asserts the equality of Aryans. (29)

> From his point of view each citizen can claim the title of Frenchman, not because he co-operates, in his place or in his occupation, with others in the economic, social, and cultural life of the nation, but because he has, in the same way as everybody else, an imprescriptible and inborn right to the indivisible totality of the country. (29)

Furthermore, the status and egalitarian nature of the us-object appears as an objective quality of the group. Yet this "egalitarianism" extends only to Aryans: all members of the Aryan elite have equivalent rights and value, and their status as the elite is affirmed through mistreatment of the Jew:

> By treating the Jew as an inferior and pernicious being, I affirm at the same time that I belong to the elite. This elite, in contrast to those of modern times which are based on merit or labor, closely resembles an aristocracy of birth. There is nothing I have to do to merit my superiority, and neither can I lose it. It is given once and for all. It is a *thing*. (27)

Thus, through his membership of an us-object, the anti-Semite secures for himself a social position, a social attitude, and a life project that is ready-made for him. It is his, from which he reaps benefits, yet he bears no responsibility for it. His is a social position unearned, an attitude to self and others that is attributed as having come from the outside, imposed from some mystical nature of things, and a project that is both his (when rewards are to be dealt out) and not his (when accountability is demanded).

We have seen how one can interpret the anti-Semite's identification with a group in terms of the us-object. However such an interpretation raises an intriguing question. If the anti-Semite exists as part of an us-object, who or what acts as the third, that all-important subject that constitutes the us-object through its gaze? One possible candidate for the position of third is the Jew. At one point in *Anti-Semite and Jew*

Sartre claims that the anti-Semite "has chosen to find his being entirely outside himself, never to look within, to be nothing save the fear he inspires in others" (21). This "being entirely outside of himself" surely refers to the anti-Semite's facticity, his being an object-for-others of which, I have suggested, his membership in an us-object constitutes an important part. In this passage it is those who are afraid of the anti-Semite that constitute the anti-Semite as an object. Here, Sartre's theory of emotion can come into play. In *The Emotions: Outline of a Theory*, emotions such as fear are described as ways in which a subject apprehends an *object* as being, in this case, fearful. Thus, those who fear the anti-Semite may be those that produce the fearful, anti-Semite us-object.[22]

While at times it might be the case that the anti-Semite's us-object is constituted by the look of a victim, there is a problem with designating the role of third to the Jew, at least as an enduring third. The problem is that while the anti-Semite in his bad faith experiences himself as an essence-driven object, he perceives the Jew in a similar way. In the anti-Semite's Manichaean worldview, both "the Aryan" and "the Jew" are governed by their respective racial essences. Thus both "the Jew" and the anti-Semite exist as objects in the anti-Semite's world, and if the anti-Semite ignores "the Jew's" subjectivity, the anti-Semite cannot experience "the Jew" as the third.

So who or what might take this role? It is my contention that recognition of the religious or pseudo-religious nature of the anti-Semitism that Sartre describes suggests that there exists an imaginary, supernatural entity in the anti-Semite's universe that acts as the "ultimate third." It is clear through much of *Anti-Semite and Jew* that the anti-Semite experiences himself as having some mystical link to the homeland and a duty to his race that carry with them spiritual connotations. For example: "The anti-Semite can conceive only of a type of primitive ownership of land based on a veritable magical rapport, in which the thing possessed and its possessor are united by a bond of mystical participation."[23] And, more suggestively:

> Knight-errant of the Good, the anti-Semite is a holy man. The Jew also is holy in his manner—holy like the untouchables, like savages under the interdict of taboo. Thus conflict is raised to a religious plane, and the end of the combat can be nothing other than a holy destruction. (43)

It is, then, perhaps of no small significance that Sartre uses the religious term *Manichaeism* to describe the anti-Semite's worldview.

Anti-Semitism appears as a religious crusade. If that is the case, in whose name is it being fought? Depending upon the anti-Semite in question it could be God (Sartre sometimes refers to the anti-Semite as "Christian"[24]) or it could be something less definite. When Sartre describes the anti-Semite as an "Aryan" or a "true Frenchman" he clearly refers to the group of which the anti-Semite takes himself to be a part. In such a case it would not necessarily be God, at least not in the sense in which God is typically conceived, that is the "entity" in the service of whom the anti-Semite fights. Rather, it may be a less defined spirit, such as the "spirit of Aryanness," or the "destiny of the true people," that is at play.

In *Being and Nothingness* Sartre discusses the experience of being a part of an us-object constituted by an unrealizable, supernatural (that is, distinct from humanity) third:

> There can exist an abstract, unrealizable project of the for-itself toward an absolute totalization of itself and of *all* Others. This effort at recovering the human totality can not take place without positing the existence of a Third, who is on principle distinct from humanity and in whose eyes humanity is wholly object. . . . He is the one who in no case can enter into community with any human group, the Third in relation to whom no other can constitute himself as a third. This concept is the same as that of the being-who-looks-at and who can never be looked-at; that is, it is one with the idea of God.[25]

The anti-Semite's Manichaeism, which reduces the human world to an interplay between racial essences, stands as a clear example of a project in which a for-itself aims "toward an absolute totalization of itself and of *all* Others." Within Manichaeism all people become comprehensible in terms of limited categories. It has also been suggested thus far that the religious or mystical nature of anti-Semitism points to some spirit under whose gaze the anti-Semite (and "the Jew") is constituted.

In the passage just quoted we see Sartre claiming that a project of totalizing humanity requires such a third. It is important to note, however, that Sartre claims here that the totalization of mankind is not *constituted* by this "ultimate third." Rather, it is a requirement of a project of totalization of humanity that such a third be *posited*. Thus the project of totalization comes prior to the third. However, those participating in the project will, in their bad faith, reverse the order of priority. For them it is the experience of this third that gives them the project. There is a parallel here with the anti-Semite's reversal of priority in taking his emotion as passion. The anti-Semite constitutes "the Jew" as a hateful object through emotion, but instead experiences this emotion as being passion, such that "the Jew" is a hateful object from the start, and "the Jew" and "the Jew's" nature cause the anti-Semite's hatred. In the case of an us-object employing a supernatural third, the third is experienced as existing prior to, and constituting, the us-object's project of totalization, when in fact it is through the for-itself's project of totalization that the third is posited.

But the us-object has been defined as an object that emerges as the result of the self and others falling under the gaze of a third. Can the concept of the us-object accommodate a scenario in which there is no real third? Yes it can, because, as we saw earlier, Sartre allows that one may experience being-for-others in the absence of any actually existing other: "He who has once been for-others is contaminated in his being for the rest of his days" (412). In a similar vein, Sartre writes, concerning the us-object:

> Just as the look is only the concrete manifestation of the original fact of my existence for others, just as therefore I experience myself existing for the Other outside any individual appearance of a look, so it is not necessary that a concrete look should penetrate and transfix us in order for us to be able to experience ourselves as integrated outside in an "Us." . . . Thus whether in the presence or in the absence of the Third I can always apprehend myself either as pure selfness or as integrated in an "Us." (420)

Thus Sartre allows that one can experience oneself as being part of an us-object without any actual third being present. Importantly, this leaves open the possibility of the construction of an imaginary third to act as the foil to the self-generated us-object of the anti-Semite. This is not to say that being-for-others is itself imaginary; the facticity, particularly the embodiment, of the for-itself guarantees its openness to being-for-others as a constant and real possibility. No doubt developmentally, this experience of the self's externality and accessibility to the gaze of an other is achieved through experiences of real others. But it seems that once this capacity is formed, actual others, right here and right now, in all their particularity, become somewhat unnecessary. In cases in which being-for-others is experienced in the absence of an actual other, "the Other" is part of a formal, rather than an ontological, category, though the formal other is parasitic on a past, existing other.

While the absence of an other can be replaced by the positing of a formal, imaginary other, the other side of the coin here is that so too can an *actual* other be replaced by a formal, imaginary other. Surely this is a good way of casting the status of "the Jew" in the anti-Semite's Manichaean world. The anti-Semite projects onto an actual Jew the image of "the Jew." The actual Jew's particularities are not used to build the anti-Semite's image of "the Jew," but they act merely as confirmations for the image: either through their alleged correspondence with the image or by standing as exceptions that prove rules.

The case of the anti-Semite stands as an example of oppression in which the oppressor engages in the type of bad faith characterized by a denial of transcendence and/or an identification with facticity. In chapter 3 we saw how this worked on the level of the individual anti-Semite and how it affected the way in which the anti-Semite faced and structured the world. With the notion of the us-object we have been able to extend the analysis from the anti-Semite as a lone individual to the anti-Semite as part of a group. However, despite this shift in the level of analysis, the general type of bad faith involved remains consistent throughout. In the examination of the anti-Semite, both as an individual and as part of a group, there appears at work that type of bad faith characterized by a flight from transcendence.

In the next chapter I will examine an example of sexism. In this example the oppressor will be seen to engage in the other form of bad faith, which is characterized by a for-itself distancing itself from its facticity. This type of bad faith will be in evidence both at the level of one-to-one intersubjectivity and on the collective level upon which the oppressor will be seen to be part of a we-subject.

NOTES

1. Sartre, *Being and Nothingness*, 259.

2. At least it does so originally. As will be claimed later, the experience of being-for-others need not always require the actual presence of an other.

3. Sartre, *Being and Nothingness*, 254.

4. Arthur C. Danto, *Sartre*, 102. It should be noted that Sartre thinks that pride is an inauthentic derivative of shame. Pride is necessarily a mode of bad faith as "in order to be proud of *being that*, I must of necessity first resign myself to *being only that*" (Sartre, *Being and Nothingness*, 290). Thomas Anderson also questions Sartre's ignoring the possibility of the other's look as not being hostile: "Surely I can be the object of a caring, generous look as well as a hostile, alienating stare" (Anderson, *Sartre's Two Ethics*, 35).

5. It must be noted that this does not make the experience of being-for-others a matter of reflection. When a for-itself experiences its being-for-others it does so as unreflective consciousness of itself as an object for an other. "The unreflective consciousness does not apprehend the *person* directly or as *its* object; the person is presented to consciousness *in so far as the person is an object for the Other*. This means that all of a sudden I am conscious of myself as escaping myself, not in that I am the foundation of my own nothingness but in that I have my foundation outside of myself" (Sartre, *Being and Nothingness*, 260). In the case of reflective consciousness, however, it is the for-itself as it is for-itself, that is, the for-itself interpreted from the standpoint of the for-itself, rather than the standpoint of the other.

6. Sartre, *Being and Nothingness*, 57–58.

7. Note that it is the *synthesis* of these two modes of being that Sartre thinks impossible. In the human subject one finds both modes of being, but they are still distinct, though ambiguously related. For Sartre, authenticity involves the *coordination* of transcendence and facticity, not their synthesis.

8. Sartre, *Being and Nothingness*, 362.

9. One may, of course, pursue the two desires alternately and, as we will see, this is precisely what Sartre thinks one does.

10. Sartre, *Being and Nothingness*, 363.

11. Fuller accounts of the "radical conversion" appear in several sources, including Thomas C. Anderson, *The Foundation and Structure of Sartrean Ethics*, and Ronald E. Santoni, *Bad Faith, Good Faith*.

12. Sartre later claimed that "*Being and Nothingness* is an ontology before conversion," that is, before the conversion from the God project and bad faith to authenticity (Sartre, *Notebooks for an Ethics*, 6).

13. Sartre, *Being and Nothingness*, 415.

14. The us-object is unstable in that the for-itself could always objectify its companions in the us-object, thereby aligning itself with the third, or could return the gaze of the third, thereby reasserting its subjectivity.

15. Sartre, *Being and Nothingness*, 429.

16. "It is clear, in fact, that it [the we-subject] could not constitute an ontological structure of human reality" (Sartre, *Being and Nothingness*, 414).

17. Sartre, *Being and Nothingness*, 413.

18. It should be noted that *Anti-Semite and Jew* was not written with a philosophical audience in mind, and contains little of Sartre's technical terminology.

19. Sartre, *Anti-Semite and Jew*, 22.

20. Sartre, *Being and Nothingness*, 418.

21. Sartre, *Anti-Semite and Jew*, 26.

22. Of course those who fear the anti-Semite might include people other than Jews. In my experience of witnessing skinhead gangs in public places, it seems clear that it is not only "migrants" they wish to intimidate. However, we will assume for the moment that it is the Jew that constitutes the anti-Semite us-object through her or his fear. It is the anti-Semite as an *anti-Semite*, rather than simply a thug who hates Jews and might hurt non-Jews as well, that we are interested in here.

23. Sartre, *Anti-Semite and Jew*, 23–24.

24. For example, "the same action carried out by a Jew and by a Christian does not have the same meaning in the two cases" (Sartre, *Anti-Semite and Jew*, 34).

25. Sartre, *Being and Nothingness*, 422–23.

5

Sado-Sexism and
the Flight from Facticity

In this chapter a type of sexism, characterized by an objectification of women's bodies by the sexist, will be examined. Several feminist philosophers have written about sexism in this way, sometimes explicitly employing early Sartrean philosophy as an analytical tool.[1] Such works typically focus on the target of sexism, the woman's experience of the patriarchal gaze, and her possible complicity in her oppression. The most famous of these is Beauvoir's existentialist analysis of women's oppression in *The Second Sex*. However, unlike Beauvoir, my primary interest (as it has been throughout) is in the position of the oppressor rather than the oppressed, in this case the source of the gaze rather than the object of the gaze. It is by virtue of this focus that my analysis differs from Beauvoir's.[2]

The investigation will go as follows. First, I will examine in some detail sadism, which, as we saw in the last chapter, is one of the concrete relations with others in which the for-itself attempts to flee its facticity through the objectification of the other. Sadism refuses ambiguity in favor of an unattainable, unsituated, or pure transcendence. Second, I will discuss the operation of female beauty ideals, interpreting this phenomenon in terms of sadism. Third, having presented an account of what I call sado-sexism in terms of one-to-one intersubjectivity, I will go on to shift the analysis to the social level, where sado-sexists can be seen to act with others as a we-subject against individual women or women as a group.

SADISM, GRACE, AND OBSCENITY

It will be recalled that sadism is one of the concrete relations with others that is conducted within the second attitude toward one's being an object for another. As such, it involves the for-itself fleeing its being-for-others in some way. Of sadism, Sartre writes:

> The sadist's effort is to ensnare the Other in his flesh by means of violence and pain, by appropriating the Other's body in such a way that he treats it as flesh so as to cause flesh to be born. But this appropriation surpasses the body which it appropriates, for its purpose is to possess the body only in so far as the Other's freedom has been ensnared within it.[3]

The sadist attempts to appropriate the other's freedom, in order that the sadist may exist as pure freedom, thereby escaping the human condition: "Sadism is a refusal to be incarnated and a flight from all facticity" (399). The sadist attempts this by *incarnating* the other's freedom. This entails causing the other's consciousness to become fascinated by his[4] own body or, in other words, to have his body act as the preeminent object of his consciousness. This is brought about by the infliction of pain upon the body: "In pain facticity invades the consciousness."[5] The sadist inflicts pain through the use of instruments. The sadist wants to appear as pure freedom, in no way as an object, and hence uses instruments rather than his own body toward that end. Sartre writes: "The sadist refuses his own flesh at the same time that he uses instruments to reveal by force the Other's flesh to him. . . . [Sadism] enjoys being a free appropriating power confronting a freedom captured by the flesh" (399).

One question that comes to mind at this point is whether or not this scheme flies somewhat in the face of the existentialist concept of embodiment. Sartre shares the view, now associated especially with Merleau-Ponty,[6] that the subject is bodily. For example, Sartre holds that "being-for-itself must be wholly body and it must be wholly consciousness; it cannot be *united* with a body."[7] They cannot be united because unification implies initial separation. Sartre's way of thinking of the body would seem to make it the case that possession of an other's body entails possession of the other's consciousness. So why, then, must the sadist *incarnate* the other's consciousness? Surely the other's consciousness is already incarnate. In order to understand this we must refer to Sartre's concepts of *grace* and *obscenity*.

"In grace," Sartre says, "the body appears as a psychic being in situation" (400). In a graceful act the body disappears behind the activity. Sartre gives a prime example of this by describing the grace of a naked dancer:

> The supreme coquetry and the supreme challenge of grace is to exhibit the body unveiled with no clothing, with no veil except grace itself. The most graceful body is the naked body whose acts enclose it with an invisible garment while entirely disrobing its flesh, while the flesh is totally present to the eyes of the spectator. (400–401)

The dancer's body is in our field of vision and his or her nakedness is there to be seen. But we do not see it because although we are, in a sense, looking at the body, it is the body's movements that are the object of our gaze. It is the body as action, as story, as emotion that we see, not the body as naked flesh. The graceful body is for-itself: a body-in-situation, it is flesh as freedom. So, in the case of the graceful body, it could be said that consciousness is incarnate. But this is not the sort of incarnate consciousness that the sadist is after. The sadist's interests lie in the obscene body.

Obscenity is the opposite of *grace*. "The obscene appears when the body adopts postures which entirely strip it of its acts and which reveal the inertia of its flesh" (401). The obscene body is an object in the world, it is in-itself; it is flesh as flesh. The movements of the obscene body appear to the observer to be the result of outside forces such as gravity and simple mechanical interactions. Sartre illustrates this point as follows:

> The sight of a naked body from behind is not obscene. But certain involuntary waddlings of the rump are obscene. This is because then it is only the legs which are acting for the walker, and the rump is like an isolated cushion which is carried by the legs and the balancing of which is a pure obedience to the laws of weight. . . . It has the passivity of a thing and . . . is made to rest like a thing upon the legs. (401)

Through the use of instruments, particularly the ropes that bind the other, the sadist forces the other's body to exist in the obscene mode. It is in this obscene body that the sadist wants the other's consciousness to be invested. If successful, the sadist experiences himself as pure transcendence in opposition to the other who is obscene, inert flesh.

The obscene body that the sadist seeks to generate is the body as an object in the midst of the world. However, such a body cannot be generated in actuality, unless perhaps the other is killed, which is not the aim of sadism. Sadism is a mode of intersubjectivity. While at times Sartre gives the impression that obscenity is an objective quality of the body of the other, I suggest that obscenity is best understood as a matter of interpretation on the part of the sadist. The sadist interprets the other's body as having been rendered a flesh-object, and holds that the other too experiences his (the other's) body as being such an object. It may or may not be the case that the other actually does experience his body in this way. Either way, the obscenity of the body should be understood as an interpreted, rather than an objective, quality of the body. It will be important to keep this in mind through the following discussion.

Why is it that it is so crucial to the sadist that he force (or, rather, believe[8] that he has forced) the other to adopt the obscene mode of bodily being? While Sartre does not explicitly address this, it is possible to construct an answer to this question through reference to the doctrine of the intentionality of consciousness. We saw in chapter 1 that an important aspect of consciousness is that it is intentional. Consciousness itself is inherently empty, existing only as a relation to something else: its object. Consciousness is always consciousness *of* something. It seems reasonable to assume that this is why the simple capture of a body is not enough to capture a consciousness, even though consciousness may be embodied. To capture a consciousness, one must also have the object of that consciousness. Thus in order to capture a consciousness by way of taking the body, one must ensure that the body is the object of that consciousness.

In the case of the graceful body, the body in the mode of being-for-itself, one certainly finds consciousness and body, but the body is in no way the object for that consciousness. On the contrary, the grace-

ful body is consciousness in the world and is itself intentional, requiring some object in the world in order to exist as such. The obscene body, however, can act as an object of consciousness (both for
the sadist and the other), and this is why it is crucial for the sadist that
the other's body exists in that mode.

Evidence in support of this interpretation comes from Sartre's statement that the sadist makes the other's body "present in pain. In pain
facticity invades consciousness, and ultimately the reflective consciousness is fascinated by the facticity of the unreflective consciousness."[9] Earlier in *Being and Nothingness* Sartre claims that the body is
the facticity of the unreflective consciousness (330), and so it is reasonable to interpret this passage as saying that the sadist causes the
other to become reflectively conscious of his (the other's) own body.
The other experiences his body as an object that is being acted upon
by the sadist.[10]

The passage just quoted is an interesting one because it indicates
another element of sadism. While the reflective consciousness is positional and so always posits an object that it itself is not, the object
posited *is the self* in the mode of not being itself. Another way of putting this is to say that the object of reflective consciousness is the self
in the mode of being *me* as opposed to being *I*. Sartre writes that the
sadist forces the other's "freedom freely to identify itself with the tor-
tured flesh."[11] On this level, the other exists as being-object-for-
others. His presence in the world is as a body-object. In this sense he
is his body, but he is so in the mode of not being it. This is the human
condition: that ambiguous relation between being, on the one hand,
what one is and, on the other hand, not being what one is. In this
case, the ambiguity is manifested in the other being, on the one hand,
that body upon which the sadist is acting, and on the other hand, not
being the body that is an object for the other's consciousness. The important point here is that sadism presupposes that in neither of these
modes of the other's being can the sadist be object for the other. To
the extent that the other identifies himself as being his body as object,
he cannot transcend the transcendence of the sadist. To the extent
that the other is subject, by virtue of having his body so forcefully
present as object to his consciousness, he is in no position to objectify the sadist.

The aim of sadism is to gain for the sadist the position of being pure transcendence, avoiding any objectification by the other, and thereby escaping the human condition. But sadism is a failure. In so far as the sadist wishes to divert and appropriate the transcendent freedom of the other, the sadist finds that it is on principle beyond his reach. Where the sadist was seemingly acting upon the other's transcendence, he was in fact dealing with a transcendence transcended. The sadist "can act upon the [Other's] freedom only by making it an objective property of the Other-as-object" (405). As such, the sadist misses the mark, and "discovers his error when his victim *looks* at him; that is when the sadist experiences the absolute alienation of his being in the Other's freedom" (405). Apart from sadism's inevitable failure, as an attempted escape from facticity (in this case that arising from being-for-others) sadism stands as an example of that type of bad faith characterized by a flight from facticity.

SADISM AND FEMALE BEAUTY IDEALS

So far we have seen what the sadistic strategy entails, the important role that the concepts of grace and obscenity play in that strategy, and that, although it is a failure, the strategy is one of bad faith, aimed at maintaining the freedom of the sadist. What I now want to do is demonstrate that a number of parallels can be drawn between Sartre's account of sadism and the way in which female beauty ideals operate and affect women in our society.

We are inundated daily by images, visual images in particular, from the mass media.[12] These images carry with them societal norms regarding the way in which people are supposed to be,[13] and there is surely no stronger and no more defined a norm than that regarding the way in which women's bodies are supposed to look. Women who do not match up to this norm are often portrayed as being sad, farcical, evil, or even just downright offensive. As the media portrays itself as a mirror to reality, the message to women is loud and clear: conform to these norms or suffer the consequences.[14]

Messages portraying the female body as an object that must be attended to proliferate in the media in advertisements, talk shows, lifestyle programs, and even current affairs shows. There are a vast number of aspects of women's bodies that are indicated as requiring attention, including lines, wrinkles, bulges, body hair, and so on. Messages concerning these aspects of women's bodies are usually in the form of directives; in order to increase one's value as a woman one must ensure that. . . . By doing so, a woman is assured of coming closer to the ideal, of increasing her value.

It is not simply through explicit directives such as these that women are told to experience their bodies as conglomerations of potentially improvable problem areas. The "ideal women" of the media are seen to have overcome, or simply not have, these problems, and this is another way in which women are shown that they have work to do to "improve" their bodies. Given the backdrop of strongly and widely held values concerning the worth of women's bodies as objects, women's bodies are often viewed as objects awaiting assessment. Thus, although the "ideal women" in the media may well be doing things, it is not as active bodies that we are to admire them. It is their bodies as gradable parts that we are to assess, and these bodies are used as the standards by which other women's bodies are assessed. It is ironic that the ideal body should be judged as an object isolatable from action when we consider that what gives it its ideal shape and texture may be its similarity in appearance to an active athletic body. In fact, for all intents and purposes, a woman is required to be an athlete in order to achieve the correct body form. But it is not in the midst of such athletic activity that a woman's body is to be admired. It is after the fact of having achieved that shape that the female body is admired, as obscene flesh.[15]

This ideal form is difficult to achieve, and the requirement upon women to conform to it might make many women invest a great deal of their attention to their bodies. Those that have achieved the required shape and texture have worked and concentrated hard on doing so, and must continue to work and concentrate hard on maintaining it. But it is not only those women, with bodies corresponding to the ideal, that might be interpreted by an observer as having their consciousness invested in their bodies. To think so would be to underestimate the pervasiveness of the ideal. Women who are, according to the prevailing standards, too fat or too thin, too short or too tall, too old or too young, would be constantly reminded of their own bodies by their deviation from the ideal that is everywhere flaunted, valued, and worshipped. They too would have their consciousness invested in their bodies. Their bodies would always be present as an object of their consciousness, even for the reason that they realize that their bodies do not conform to the ideal, and with the pervasiveness of the images carrying that message, this realization must be a difficult one to avoid.[16]

A number of parallels can be drawn between Sartre's account of sadism and the operation of female beauty ideals. In sadism, the other's body is made to exist in the obscene mode through the activities of the sadist, which strip it of grace. Gila Hayim describes the obscene body in sadism as being the "body as constituted of isolated parts, and as a thing unrelated to the situation."[17] The female beauty ideal demands that women's bodies adopt the obscene mode of being by way of making their bodies, as objects, as "constituted of isolated parts," a cause for concern. The ideal body as an object for perusal and assessment has certain properties and, as an ideal that carries some weight by virtue of its being generally accepted, stands as a value demanding fulfillment. The message is clear and, due to its continual transmission, it cannot help but be received by many women. Thus, female beauty ideals set women up to view their bodies as being objects for themselves and others. But recall that the sadist does not merely set the other up to experience his (the other's) body as object. The sadist, through the infliction of pain, makes the other's body demand attention. In the issue of female beauty ideals it is the continual and pervasive nature of the ideal, or messages transmitting it, in conjunction with the persuasive nature of general attitudes toward it, that command women to experience their bodies as objects, often even as the preeminent object of their consciousness. It is this that parallels the sadist's infliction of pain upon the other's body, as a way to make the body, as flesh, demand the attention of the other's consciousness. In short, the institution of female beauty ideals parallels the procedures of Sartre's sadist, in that both aim at "the other" experiencing their bodies as objects of their own consciousness.

Thus far parallels have been drawn between sadism and female beauty ideals on the basis of their similarity with respect to their operations on the target or object of the respective procedures. But pointing to similarities between these effects is neither sufficient to make the claim that there may be something sadistic about female beauty ideals, nor is it the aspect of the issue that I wish to address. Rather, the claim that I want to make is that to be a man in our society is to have the possibility of adopting a position, in relation to the structures of beauty ideals, that parallels that of the sadist.

SADISM AND MALE INVISIBILITY

Could there be something sadistic (in the Sartrean sense) about the position achieved by men with respect to women through the institution of female beauty ideals? In other words, does the institution of beauty ideals share structures in common with sadism in terms of the subject/object arrangement that it puts in place? It would be necessary to establish two states of affairs in order to provide an affirmative answer. The first is that men might experience women as being bodies in the mode of objects, with their (the women's) consciousness limited to intending their own bodies. The second is that men might experience their own bodies as not being objects in the world to be looked at, and that this arrangement would not be what it is without the foil provided by the converse arrangement faced by women.

These two conditions for the possibility of designating men as taking up a position structurally similar to that of the sadist with respect to women, through the institution of female beauty ideals, can be supported through reference to two observations concerning our society and its obsession with women's physical appearance. The first observation is that there is a masculine/feminine dichotomy in operation in society, through which *woman* is defined in opposition to *man*.[18] One of the clearest formulations of this idea emerges from Nancy Jay's "Gender and Dichotomy." Here Jay claims that "there is, in every society a dichotomous distinction: that between male and female . . . [which tends to be] phrased in terms of A and Not-A."[19] Jay links this phrasing in terms of A and not-A to the Aristotelian logical principles of contradiction (nothing can be both A and not-A) and the excluded middle (all things are either A or not-A) (92–93). Furthermore, she emphasizes that the male side of the dichotomy is the positive (A) side, and the female side the negative (not-A) side. Hence, within such a dichotomous arrangement, male qualities have priority so that that which is female is that which is not male. Hélène Cixous, on a similar track, lists a number of binary pairs of characteristics (which she describes as "dual hierarchical oppositions")[20] accorded to men and women respectively on each side of the masculine/feminine dichotomy. These include (with the masculine characteristic appearing first) activity/passivity, culture/nature, head/heart, and logos/pathos (37). Again, the "logic" of the dichotomy results in feminine traits being those that are not masculine, and of negative value.

The second observation is that our society places disproportionate emphasis on female beauty. In connection to this greater emphasis placed on women's appearance, Naomi Wolf refers to what she calls the "beauty myth." This myth tells a story in which "the quality called 'beauty' objectively and universally exists. Women must want to embody it and men must want to possess women who embody it. This embodiment is an imperative for women and not for men."[21] Women are valued in reference to their physical appearance both more generally and more fundamentally than are men. In saying that the standards of physical appearance are applied more *fundamentally* to women than to men, I mean that her value as a woman is more closely tied to physical appearance than is a man's value as a man. In saying that standards of physical appearance are applied more *generally* to women than to men I mean that women in general, regardless of context, will be judged more often with respect to their physical appearance than will men. Certainly, there is an ideal for male beauty, but its application seems to be limited to particular contexts. While it may be commonplace for men such as actors, models, and entertainers to be looked at and appraised in terms of their physical appeal, it would appear out of place to do this to other men. Women's bodies, however, are considered appropriate objects of perusal and judgment with respect to prevailing standards of beauty in almost any context. Even in politics, an arena in which clashes of personality and ideology might be considered definitive, it is far from rare for journalists or other media figures to allude to a female politician's figure, dress, or hairstyle. Similar reporting of a male politician's appearance would come across as being a joke.

One of the effects of a society, or a section of society, placing disproportionate emphasis on the appearance of women's bodies in comparison to the emphasis placed on the appearance of men's bodies, is that it tends to make men's bodies less visible, less noticeable. This is a consequence of the strong association that is made between beauty requirements and femininity, in conjunction with the prevailing masculine/feminine dichotomy. Through this dichotomy the importance of men's bodies as objects for perusal becomes inversely proportional to the importance of women's bodies as objects to be looked at.[22] Thus, I suggest, we can add to Cixous's list of binary pairs the pair (masculine) bodily absence/(feminine) bodily presence. It must be stressed, however, that in the current context *bodily presence* refers merely to the body's presence as an appropriate object for perusal, while *bodily absence* refers to the body's inappropriateness as such an object. Of course, both men and women have bodies with material existence in the world, bodies that could always be looked at. Thus, the claim that men are accorded relative invisibility through the dichotomy means that *they tend not to be seen* (in the relevant sense) rather than it being literally impossible to see them.

An example of what I mean by the relative invisibility gained by men through prevailing standards of physical appearance can emerge from a consideration of what, in many Western cultures, constitutes appropriate modes of dressing for men and women on formal occasions, such as balls or formal dinners. At social events like these, women are expected to wear a dress, men a suit. For the women's dresses, the possible styles, fabrics, colors, and patterns are only loosely limited. While the dresses must all be very "feminine," they must never be the same. Surely there is no greater embarrassment for a woman than to turn up to a ball to find that she is wearing the same dress as someone else (at least, that is what the movies tell us). The women, clothed in different colors and styles, catch the eye. They are meant to be looked at. For the men, however, the situation is quite the opposite. They are supposed to dress more or less the same as each other. Formal men's attire is quite uniform, with only very minor deviations being acceptable. Although the men look nice in their formal attire, they all look very much alike, and with this uniformity goes a kind of invisibility or anonymity. None is supposed to stand out from the others and, as the strict structuring of such events gives a certain imperativeness to the whole affair, the message here would seem to be that individual men *should not* be looked at. While the men can look at the women (who are presented as being there to be looked at), the anonymity of the herd afforded by the men's uniform gives some security against being looked at themselves and, if anything, suggests that they are not to be looked at. Men are the less visible observers, women the highly visible observed.

The (masculine) bodily absence/(feminine) bodily presence dichotomy is not absolute, but rather one of emphasis. Men *tend not to* be looked at as body-objects; women *tend to* be looked at as body-objects. The recognition of the dichotomy exposes social values concerning the applicability of standards of physical appearance, standards that are applied differentially to women and men. Female beauty ideals, with their wide scope and fundamentality of application, play a role in the creation and maintenance of the bodily absence/bodily presence dichotomy. They are both a manifestation of the dichotomy and one of the means of ensuring its continued existence. Interpreted this way, female beauty ideals function as a kind of one-way mirror through which men can see women. But this seeing is non-reciprocal. All women are meant to see is an image of themselves.

This brings us back to the question that was raised at the beginning of the section: could there be something sadistic (in the sense of sharing a similar subject/object arrangement as that occurring in sadism) about the position taken up by men with respect to women through the institution of female beauty ideals? The two conditions for a positive answer were that female beauty ideals result, first, in men experiencing women as body-objects fascinated by their own objectivity and, second, in men experiencing their own bodies as not being objects that are looked at. The first condition gains support through the observation that female beauty ideals are applied fundamentally and generally to women and that there is a strong association between the importance of beauty and femininity. With social imperatives requiring that women be feminine, and with femininity being closely tied to the observance of beauty standards, there is ample scope for interpreting women as being preoccupied with their bodies-as-objects.[23] The second condition gains support through the observation that there operates a masculine/feminine dichotomy with respect to physical appearance, such that the great importance placed on feminine physical appearance translates to a much lesser importance being placed on masculine physical appearance. This, it has been argued, results in the relative invisibility of men's bodies. Through the greater emphasis placed on others-as-object, men might hope to escape their own being-for-others. As the strategy for achieving this state of not having being-for-others is to limit (or at least perceive to have limited) the consciousness of the other to the other's own body-as-flesh-object, the strategy emerges as having a similar structure to sadism.

The foregoing analysis reveals the *possibility* that female beauty ideals are employed in a project structurally similar to that of sadism and gestures toward a possible position that is there in our society for a man to occupy. If we accept that it is definitive of sadism that a subject seeks to resolve the ambiguity of the human condition by, first, escaping his or her being-for-others, and attempts to reach this state by, second, treating and objectifying the body of the other in a fashion intending that it flood the other's consciousness, thereby rendering the other unable to look at the subject, then scenarios that contain these elements can be understood as mirroring sadism. I have argued that such could be the case in situations involving beauty ideals, and have raised evidence to support this suggestion. The question of whether some men actually do experience themselves and women in this way is difficult to answer definitively in the absence of some other kind of study (sociological, psychological) that is beyond the scope of this work. However, we can say at this point that the hypothesis that there is something sadistic (in the relevant, Sartrean sense) about the institution of female beauty ideals would, in the light of the foregoing analysis, appear to be a reasonable one to propose. I will us the term *sado-sexism* to refer to instances of sexism that parallel sadism.

If it were demonstrated that (at least sometimes) female beauty ideals are employed in a male, sado-sexist project, wherein women subject to those ideals take up a position structurally similar to the other in sadism, someone might be tempted to conclude that these women are in a position that, in some ways at least, mirrors that of the masochist. However, this further claim is certainly not one I wish to make. First, my interest here is in the sadist/observer, rather than the other/observed. It is the phenomenology of oppression from the perspective of the oppressor that is the focus of my discussion, as it has been throughout.[24] Second, it is far from clear that identifying someone as the other of sadism is to identify that person as a masochist. Sadism is a project with respect to an other, the goal of which is to establish a position of pure subjectivity for the sadist. The route taken by sadism in attempting to reach this goal is the objectification and domination of the other's body, rendering it an object. To the extent that sadism is successful or maintainable at all, it is through *the sadist* experiencing (erroneously) the achievement of this objectification of the other. As such, this does not address the actual experience or motivations of the other, and it certainly does not require that the other be a masochist. Sadism does not require a masochistic other. It is the sadist's perceptions of the other and the situation that constitutes sadism, not the other's perceptions.

SADO-SEXISTS AND THE WE-SUBJECT

In making the claim that men can use female beauty in a sadistic fashion to attempt to escape their being-for-others, we have been dealing with phenomena that occur at a social or cultural level. The masculine/feminine dichotomy, for instance, is a social value. And beauty ideals themselves, by their very nature, are cultural patterns, social institutions. However, the Sartrean account of sadism is an account of one-to-one intersubjectivity, not of a social or collective enterprise. In order to recognize the social level at work in the issue of female beauty ideals, it will be necessary to recast the account thus far given in terms that are more commensurable with the sociality of the phenomenon, through reference to the sado-sexist as taking part in a we-subject.

It will be recalled from the discussion in the last chapter that the we-subject is a subject-community whose look is directed toward a shared object. In the context of the current discussion, sado-sexists can be viewed as participating in such a community with other sado-sexists, which is to say they form a we-subject. The shared object in this case is women as a them-object.[25] This, at least, is the subject/

object arrangement in the cultural pattern that is the masculine/ feminine dichotomy, which comes into play in female beauty ideals. Women are viewed as objects gradable in reference to prevailing standards of beauty. This is part of their "femininity." Men, on the other hand, are not to be viewed, in general, in this way. Rather, they are subjects; they are those who look at the women-object.

This we-subject/them-object arrangement can be at work even in a case where an individual man is in the presence of an individual woman. For the man, the woman stands, prima facie, as an object by virtue of her being a woman, and thus being a member of the women/them-object, one of the characteristics of which is to be assessable in terms of physical appearance. Also the man stands, prima facie, as subject by virtue of his membership of the men/we-subject. His status as part of the subject group gives him, initially at least, the invisibility that is sought by the sadist. I say "initially" because, in any encounter with the other, the other returning the gaze could turn the tables on the for-itself. Any invisibility gained by the for-itself in such an arrangement is, as it is with all positions pursued in bad faith, an evanescent phenomenon. Regardless of what the for-itself may do to insulate itself from its being-for-others, it will always have an outside, a bodily presence in the world that could be looked at. However, this initial position (men as lookers, women as looked at) is important, as it is this that betrays the cultural values involved with respect to physical appearance, and it is this that stands as one of the oppressive aspects of our society.

In the last chapter it was stated that Sartre's account of the we-subject made it appear as a social form of lesser significance. I argued that this was due to Sartre's discussion centering only on the we-subject as a pure form. His discussion of the bourgeoisie as a we-subject was examined, and I argued that by accepting that a we-subject will not be of a pure form, one is able to account for the greater unity that may be observed amongst the bourgeoisie than the abstract category of a pure we-subject would otherwise allow. The application of the concept of the we-subject in the case of the sado-sexist also exposes the limitations of Sartre's concept, pointing again to the need for a reformulation of it. In my example of the sado-sexist, I have needed to turn to the concept of the we-subject in order to bring the description onto the social level. This has been necessitated by my earlier reference to a masculine/feminine dichotomy at work in society and the cultural nature of beauty ideals. I have then suggested that, at least with respect to beauty ideals, the dichotomy operates to produce a masculine we-subject and a feminine them-object. But in order for such a masculine we-subject to be possible, those who constitute the we-subject must make some recognition of their own masculinity and the masculinity of their we-subject colleagues. This would seem to require something more than the for-itself's merely indirect, pre-reflective awareness of the consciousness of the other for-itselves in the we-subject, which is the only form of intra-we-subject recognition that Sartre allows. In the we-subject that we have described in the context of beauty ideals, the for-itself would have to recognize himself as belonging to the same group as the others in the we-subject, a group that, as *male*, is based on facticity. It would require both self-assessment and assessment of others.

The inconsistency between Sartre's presentation of the we-subject and my application of it lies in Sartre's presentation of the concept as the description of a pure form of the we-subject in which the we-subject is a community of consciousnesses. There can be no room for any positing of oneself or the others that help to make up the we-subject. But such a pure form is impossible, as it would require the successful shedding of facticity, which is an inescapable aspect of the human condition. That is, at least partly, why aiming toward such a state as the pure we-subject is a form of bad faith. The human condition is an ambiguous combination of transcendence and facticity. As much as someone may attempt to reach a state of pure transcendence she will always carry her facticity with her and, along with her facticity, her being-for-others. What was true for the sadist (namely, his failure to attain the position of pure subject) is every bit as true for the we-subject. While it may be argued that men hold a position of we-subject against a women/them-object, this position can never be attained in a pure form. The very fact that the we-subject is male belies its impurity, referring, as it must do, to considerations regarding facticity.

However, holding that the male we-subject is not a pure we-subject does not diminish the importance of the diagnosis, but rather underscores the bad faith with respect to both self and others that it involves. Nor does the postulation of an impure we-subject diminish the fact that the creation and maintenance of such a structure may lead to oppression when the we-subject's shared object is other people. On the contrary, the internal inconsistency of the male we-subject, in its making a claim to pure subjectivity for a group based, at least in part, on elements of facticity, requires constant reinforcement through continual objectification of women in its attempt to maintain itself. Thus, while the goal of the we-subject may be on principle unattainable and in vain, its impact may be all too real.

Having recast the analysis of men's position due to female beauty ideals in terms of the we-subject in order to accommodate the sociality of the phenomenon, are we able to speak of the we-subject as sadistic, in the relevant sense of that term? After all, Sartre's account of sadism is of a one-to-one intersubjective arrangement. I think we can extend his account of sadism to the social realm. For one, it is clear that Sartre, through the introduction of the notions of the us-object and we-subject, understood his work on intersubjectivity to be of relevance to collectivities. Furthermore, sadism, albeit a one-to-one relation with the other in Sartre's description, is at bottom just a form of objectification of the other. There seems no reason why the we-subject, as an objectifying group, should not use as its method of objectification the sadistic method (which carries the intention of treating the body of the other in such a way that it becomes the object of the other's consciousness) and if it does so it is reasonable to describe this we-subject as *sadistic*, or at least *sadist-like*.

I have claimed that a we-subject may take up a sadist-like position in opposition to its shared object. However, it is important to point out that we should not understand the we-subject as being simply a plurality of individual "sadists." It is not the case that the sado-sexist we-subject is a plurality of subjects who individually and separately, without reference to each other, take up the "right" to be observers and objectifiers of women. Rather, the "right" of each individual to objectify women comes from his membership of the male we-subject. Thus the collective has a socio-ontological status, which its members can draw from, and which they can employ in opposition to women.

Thus far I have only considered beauty ideals and dress standards, but there are other examples of social practices that set up a sadism-like arrangement in which a subject may attempt to develop a status of unambiguous transcendence, a state of unidirectional looking, through the deflection of the other's gaze away from the subject and onto their own body. Another example of sado-sexism is the practice of so-called wolf whistling. Sandra Bartky provides a vivid account of her experience of being the target of this practice:

> It is a fine spring day, and with an utter lack of self-consciousness, I am bouncing down the street. Suddenly I hear men's voices. Catcalls and whistles fill the air. These noises are clearly sexual in intent and they are meant for me; they come from across the street. I freeze. . . . My face flushes and my motions become stiff and self-conscious. The body which only a moment before I inhabited with such ease now floods my consciousness. I have been made into an object. While it is true that for these men I am nothing but, let us say, a "nice piece of ass," there is more involved in this encounter than their mere fragmented perception of me. They could, after all, have enjoyed me in silence. Blissfully un-aware, breasts bouncing, eyes on the birds in the trees, I could have passed by without having been turned to stone. But I must be *made* to know that I am a "nice piece of ass": I must be made to see myself as they see me. There is an element of compulsion in this encounter, in this being-made-to-be-aware of one's own flesh; like being made to apolo-gize, it is humiliating[26]

The scenario that Bartky describes here appears as another example of sado-sexism at work, displaying several significant similarities to the female beauty ideal scenarios described earlier. As with beauty ideals, the wolf whistle can be interpreted as aiming at bringing to a woman's attention her body as a flesh-object. It is not a matter of be-ing observed as a body in situation. Rather, it aims to strip the body of its being-in-the-world, rendering it a simple object in the world. Bartky's example also contains the element of *forcible* objectification that is a hallmark of sadism: "I must be *made* to know that I am a 'nice piece of ass': I must be made to see myself as they see me." She could have been admired at a distance, but that would not have had the ob-jectifying effect gained through forcing her to be aware of her being seen and the manner in which she is seen. Finally, there are similari-ties between the catcallers and the men who are not subject to beauty ideals. Both are rendered, in a sense, invisible. While wolf whistles may often come from dark corners of construction site scaffolding or from behind tinted car windows, such material hiding places are not necessary. Men by virtue of being men and hence not seen in terms of their body-objectness are relatively invisible. Standing from behind a screen, be it material or socially conventional, for them the world of women is a peep show.

I do not claim that all men within Western patriarchy have assumed the subject position of invisibility. On the contrary, subject positions that render the body highly visible are available to men. For example there are men (such as film and television stars) whose occupations place their bodies under scrutiny. Nor is it the case that Western patriarchy has always relied on male invisibility. For instance, artists in classical Greece celebrated men's bodies as objects of beauty, and the men of eighteenth-century French aristocracy dressed with vivid ostentation. Both societies were, nonetheless, male dominated. However, male invisibility does seem to have been fairly common in twentieth-century Western society,[27] and its further description and thematization will no doubt be valuable to understanding contemporary patriarchy.

Sado-sexism is a type of sexism that is interpretable in terms of a number of the concepts that have been examined in this book. In particular, sado-sexism involves the sado-sexist engaging in that type of bad faith characterized by a denial of facticity and identification with transcendence. On the level of one-to-one intersubjectivity, this bad faith is played out in a manner similar to sadism. The sexist attempts to insulate himself from being-for-others by objectifying the other and engaging in practices aimed at the other experiencing herself as an object. On the level of collectivity we saw the sado-sexist as part of a we-subject. It was necessary to modify Sartre's account of the we-subject somewhat, by speaking of a less than pure form that could accommodate intra-we-subject recognition of masculinity by its members. This was an important move as the masculine/feminine dichotomy was seen to be at work in setting up the subject/object arrangement paralleling sadism.

CLOSING REMARKS

My analyses of anti-Semitic racism and sado-sexism support the claim that Sartre's early philosophy is useful in interpreting at least some cases of oppression. By using concepts such as *bad faith*, *us-object*, and *we-subject*, we can make sense of an oppressor's inauthentic worldview and relations with others. Furthermore, interpreting an oppressor's approach to himself and others in this way allows us to attribute personal responsibility to him for his oppressive behaviors. He conducts himself on the basis of false beliefs, but he is not helpless with respect to them. These beliefs are not inevitable. They can be understood as motivated and pursued, rather than the results of poor information or lack of proper reasoning,[28] and they are open to change.

In the introduction I made the qualification that I would limit my focus to the oppressor, as an agent, and not to the structural aspects of oppression. As such, the approach to oppression that I have taken here can only lead to a partial understanding of the complex phenomena of oppression. However, it is important to point out that accounts of oppression that focus on structures need not be incompatible with a Sartrean approach. The Sartrean individual lives in a society that contains institutions and supports particular discourses, and this forms part of her facticity, her situation of choice. Facticity is an indispensable element of the individual and it can *condition* choice, through limiting available options. But, for Sartre, facticity cannot be seen as *determining* choice. It is only accounts of oppression that give to structures a *determining* (rather than a *conditioning*) role in the formation of beliefs and behaviors, which will immediately be incompatible with the Sartrean approach that I have presented.

Finally, there is a further clarification I wish to make with respect to oppression and the two types of bad faith. While I have discussed a case of racism involving a bad faith denial of transcendence, and a case of sexism involving a bad faith denial of facticity, it should not be thought that racism and sexism, per se, are tied to any one type of bad faith. Racism and sexism could involve either type of bad faith, and the type of bad faith involved will affect the character of the particular case of oppression under consideration.

Cases of racism, for example, can involve a bad faith denial of facticity, rather than the denial of transcendence diagnosed in chapter 3. Take for example the practice, which was at one time commonly engaged in by Australians of British descent, of referring to Australians not of British descent as "ethnics." Calling the other an "ethnic" not only draws attention to the other's ethnicity (no doubt as a form of pejorative) but also suggests that the speaker is unaware of her own ethnicity. The racist in this case does not frame her opposition to the other in terms of a clash of ethnicities, in a manner similar to the racism of the anti-Semite in *Anti-Semite and Jew*, for whom both self and other are definable in terms of their respective "racial essences." Rather, it is only the other who is "ethnic." If bad faith is to be found in this case, it will be bad faith characterized by a focus on the facticity of the other, to the exclusion of awareness of the facticity of the self. In other words, it will be bad faith as a flight from facticity, thereby making this case closer in kind to my example of sado-sexism, than to the example of the anti-Semite.

Similarly, while the sexism analyzed in this chapter was one in which bad faith as flight from facticity was involved, it should not be thought that the bad faith involved in sexism must be of this type. In contrast to the sexism in which men attempt to hold the position of genderless, invisible observer, one can also think of sexist scenarios in which the man is very much *a man*. Take for example the "boys club" type of sexism, which characterizes some pubs and workplaces, in which "we blokes have to stick together" in response to the unwelcome presence of women. Here the opposition to women is framed in terms of competing genders and, thus, the man must *clearly and reflectively* identify himself as a *man* in opposition to a *woman*. In such a case, the man's focus is on both his and the woman's facticities, to the exclusion of awareness of his and her respective subjectivities. Along with this objectification might follow notions of "gender-essences" and the requirement to protect the territory reserved for one's own group from invasion or contamination by members of another group. This case would, then, seem to involve bad faith as flight from transcendence and (in this respect) be closer in kind to the racism discussed in chapter 3 than to sado-sexism.

NOTES

1. Examples of these include Julien S. Murphy, "The Look in Sartre and Rich," and Sandra Bartky, "On Psychological Oppression," in her *Femininity and Domination*.

2. Another difference lies in my focus on Sartre's concept of bad faith. While Sartre and Beauvoir shared much in their respective philosophies, bad

faith, a much-used concept in Sartre, rarely figures in Beauvoir's work. Interestingly, Michèle Le Doeuff claims that the absence of the concept of bad faith, among other "masculinist elements in Sartre's work," in the work of Beauvoir, allows Beauvoir's "reworking of existentialism" to accommodate accounts of oppression (Le Doeuff, *Hipparchia's Choice*, 96–97). However, in contrast to this, I am arguing that bad faith is a useful concept in thematising oppression, particularly where the focus is on the oppressor.

3. Sartre, *Being and Nothingness*, 403.

4. In this exegesis I shall follow Sartre in using the masculine pronoun for both the sadist and the other.

5. Sartre, *Being and Nothingness*, 399.

6. It should be noted that Merleau-Ponty believed that Sartre's ontology did not take embodiment into account adequately. For a discussion of Merleau-Ponty's objections to Sartre, see Monika Langer, *Merleau-Ponty's Phenomenology of Perception*, 97–104. Although it may be true that Sartre did not develop an account of, or concentrate on, embodiment to the same degree as Merleau-Ponty, there is ample evidence in *Being and Nothingness* to suggest that he at least had some notion of embodiment, and that he assumed and used that notion in many of his discussions (as we saw in chapter 1).

7. Sartre, *Being and Nothingness*, 305.

8. I use the term *believe* here to mean something along the lines of: S believes p if S behaves in a manner suggesting that p is the case. This leaves open the possibility that the sadist does not reflectively hold the belief or is not reflectively aware of the full significance of his actions.

9. Sartre, *Being and Nothingness*, 399.

10. Jacques Salvan seems to be in support of this interpretation when he writes that Sartre's sadist "wants the other's consciousness to be entirely absorbed and fascinated by body-consciousness through pain" (Salvan, *To Be and Not To Be*, 96).

11. Sartre, *Being and Nothingness*, 403.

12. The analysis conducted throughout this chapter centers on recent Western culture and is not intended to provide a description of all cultures at all times.

13. I do not wish to claim that the media is the sole source of these values, merely that it is a significant transmitter and maintainer of them.

14. Susan Bordo gives a graphic description of a television talk show audience's aggressive response to an obese woman who refused to "admit" that the shape of her body made her miserable (Bordo, "Reading the Slender Body," 100).

15. Beauvoir writes: "The ideal of feminine beauty is variable, but certain demands remain constant; for one thing, since woman is destined to be possessed, her body must present the inert and passive qualities of an object. . . . Her body is not perceived as the radiation of a subjective personality, but as a thing sunk deeply in its own immanence; it is not for such a body to have reference to the rest of the world, it must not be the promise of things other than itself" (Beauvoir, *The Second Sex*, 189).

16. I am by no means claiming that all will respond to or engage with these norms in the same way, merely that *some* kind of impact seems inevitable.

17. Gila J. Hayim, *The Existential Sociology of Jean-Paul Sartre*, 47.

18. Beauvoir points to just such an arrangement when she writes: "A man is in the right in being a man; it is the woman who is in the wrong. It amounts to this: just as for the ancients there was an absolute vertical with reference to which the oblique was defined, so there is an absolute human type, the masculine" (Beauvoir, *The Second Sex*, 15).

19. Nancy Jay, "Gender and Dichotomy," 93–94.

20. Hélène Cixous, "The Newly Born Woman," 37.

21. Naomi Wolf, *The Beauty Myth*, 12.

22. Jay, in "Gender and Dichotomy," argues that the masculine/feminine dichotomy is one in which the masculine characteristic has priority, with the feminine characteristic generated through the negation of the masculine characteristic. In my argument for the relative invisibility of men I seem to be going the other way, that is, first we have emphasis on female beauty, then, through negation, we have the lesser emphasis on male appearance. However, it need not be seen this way. The body absent/body present dichotomy could be seen as a part of and a support to a more general subject/object dichotomy, where man is the transcendent and woman the immanent. As such, the emphasis upon female beauty can be seen as an effect of the project of male transcendence, a project that has priority over the project of the objectification of women, such that the project of objectification is conducted in the service of the project of transcendence.

23. I say "interpreting" because in this argument it is the perspective of the man that is at issue. It is how he views the situation of women that will determine whether or not he is a sadist. More will be said about this in the main text.

24. Examples of works dealing with women's experience of sexism using an existentialist framework, apart from those already mentioned in note 1, include Beauvoir, *The Second Sex*, and Bartky, "Narcissism, Femininity, and Alienation."

25. It should be noted that it is not necessary for a we-subject to have as its shared object a them-object. The shared object could be an individual or a material object. In the case at hand, however, the shared object is a them-object or, at least, an individual that is selected for attention by virtue of her membership of a them-object.

26. Bartky, *Femininity and Domination*, 27.

27. At least it has until the last decade or so. Since the mid-1980s there would appear to have been a shift in popular culture, a shift characterized by a renewed interest in the bodies of men as objects for perusal. Sean Nixon, who describes it as the creation of the "new man," has documented this shift, particularly as it has occurred with respect to the visual representation of men's bodies in advertising (Nixon, "Exhibiting Masculinity"). An analysis of the significance of this shift in focus for gender relations would be a most worthwhile project.

28. I do not mean to foreclose the possibility that some people who exhibit racist or sexist behaviors might do so on the basis of bad information or faulty reasoning. But if a person does not give up her beliefs in the face of relevant counterevidence, and if we cannot identify in her some kind of cognitive disability, then we need to look in the direction of a moral psychology, like that provided by Sartre, in order to understand how her beliefs have been motivated and held. Doing this, along Sartrean lines, will lead us to see her as responsible for her beliefs.

Bibliography

Anderson, Thomas C. *The Foundation and Structure of Sartrean Ethics.*
Lawrence: Regents Press of Kansas, 1979.
———. *Sartre's Two Ethics: From Authenticity to Integral Humanity.*
Chicago: Open Court, 1993.
Appiah, Kwame Anthony. "Racisms." In *Anatomy of Racism*, edited by David
Theo Goldberg, 3–17. Minneapolis: University of Minnesota Press, 1990.
Barnes, Hazel E. "Sartre on the Emotions." In *Sartre: An Investigation of
Some Major Themes*, edited by Simon Glynn, 71–85. Aldershot, Hants,
England: Avebury, 1987.
———. "Sartre's Ontology: The Revealing and Making of Being." In The
Cambridge Companion to Sartre, edited by Christina Howells, 13–38. Cam-
bridge: Cambridge University Press, 1992.
Bartky, Sandra. "Narcissism, Femininity, and Alienation." *Social Theory and
Practice* 8, no. 2 (summer 1982): 127–43.
———. *Femininity and Domination.* New York: Routledge, 1990.
Beauvoir, Simone de. *The Ethics of Ambiguity.* Translated by Bernard Frecht-
man. New York: Citadel Press, 1964.
———. *The Second Sex.* Translated and edited by H. M. Parshley. London:
Picador, 1988.
Bell, Linda. *Sartre's Ethics of Authenticity.* Tuscaloosa: University of Alabama
Press, 1989.
Berlin, Isaiah. *Four Essays on Liberty.* Oxford: Oxford University Press,
1969.

Bordo, Susan. "Reading the Slender Body." In *Body/Politics: Women and the Discourses of Science*, edited by Mary Jacobus, Evelyn Fox Keller, and Sally Shuttleworth, 83–112. New York: Routledge, 1990.

Busch, Thomas W. *The Power of Consciousness and the Force of Circumstance in Sartre's Philosophy*. Bloomington: Indiana University Press, 1990.

Catalano, Joseph S. "Successfully Lying to Oneself: A Sartrean Perspective." *Philosophy and Phenomenological Research* 1, no. 4 (June 1990): 673–93.

Cixous, Hélène. "The Newly Born Woman." In *The Hélène Cixous Reader*, edited by Susan Sellers, translated by Betsy Wing, 37–46. London: Routledge, 1994.

Cooper, David E. *Existentialism: A Reconstruction*. Oxford: Basil Blackwell, 1990.

Cumming, Robert D. "Role-Playing: Sartre's Transformation of Husserl's Phenomenology." In *The Cambridge Companion to Sartre*, edited by Christina Howells, 39–66. Cambridge: Cambridge University Press, 1992.

Danto, Arthur C. *Sartre*. London: Fontana Press, 1985.

Descartes, René. *Meditations on First Philosophy with Selections from the Objections and Replies*. Edited and translated by John Cottingham. Cambridge: Cambridge University Press, 1996.

Detmer, David. *Freedom as a Value: A Critique of the Ethical Theory of Jean-Paul Sartre*. La Salle, Ill.: Open Court, 1986.

Fell, Joseph P. *Emotion in the Thought of Sartre*. New York: Columbia University Press, 1965.

Garcia, J. L. A. "The Heart of Racism." *Journal of Social Philosophy* 27, no. 1 (spring 1996): 5–46.

Goldberg, David Theo. "Racist Exclusions." *The Philosophical Forum* 26, no. 1 (fall 1994): 1–32.

Gordon, Lewis. *Bad Faith and Anti-Black Racism*. Atlantic Highlands, N.J.: Humanities Press, 1995.

Haight, M. R. *A Study of Self-Deception*. Brighton, Sussex: Harvester Press, 1980.

Hammond, Michael, Jane Howarth, and Russell Keat. *Understanding Phenomenology*. Oxford: Blackwell, 1991.

Hayim, Gila J. *The Existential Sociology of Jean-Paul Sartre*. Amherst: University of Massachusetts Press, 1980.

James, William. *The Principles of Psychology*. Chicago: William Benton, 1952.

Jay, Nancy. "Gender and Dichotomy." In *A Reader in Feminist Knowledge*, edited by Sneja Gunew, 89–106. London: Routledge, 1991.

Johnston, Mark. "Self-Deception and the Nature of Mind." In *Perspectives on Self-Deception*, edited by Brian P. McLaughlin and Amélie Oksenberg Rorty, 63–91. Berkeley and Los Angeles: University of California Press, 1988.

Langer, Monika. *Merleau-Ponty's Phenomenology of Perception*. London: Macmillan, 1989.

Le Doeuff, Michèle. *Hipparchia's Choice: An Essay Concerning Women, Philosophy, etc.* Translated by Trista Selous. Oxford: Blackwell, 1991.

———. "Operative Philosophy: Simone de Beauvoir and Existentialism." In *Critical Essays on Simone de Beauvoir*, edited by Elaine Marks, translated by Colin Gordon, 144–54. Boston: G. K. Hall & Co., 1987.

Matthews, Eric. *Twentieth-Century French Philosophy*. Oxford: Oxford University Press, 1996.

McCulloch, Gregory. *Using Sartre: An Analytical Introduction to Early Sartrean Themes*. New York: Routledge, 1994.

Mele, Alfred R. *Irrationality: An Essay on Akrasia, Self-Deception, and Self-Control*. Oxford: Oxford University Press, 1987.

Merleau-Ponty, Maurice. *Adventures of the Dialectic*. Translated by Joseph Bien. Evanston, Ill.: Northwestern University Press, 1973.

Mirvish, Adrian. "Gestalt Mechanisms and Believing Beliefs: Sartre's Analysis of the Phenomenon of Bad Faith." *Journal of the British Society for Phenomenology* 18, no. 3 (October 1987): 245–62.

———. "Sartre and the Gestaltists: Demystifying (Part of) *Being and Nothingness*." *Journal of the British Society for Phenomenology* 11, no. 3 (October 1980): 207–24.

———. "Sartre on Perception and the World." *Journal of the British Society for Phenomenology* 14, no. 2 (May 1983): 158–74.

Moi, Toril. *Simone de Beauvoir: The Making of an Intellectual Woman*. Oxford: Blackwell, 1994.

Monasterio, Xavier O. "The Body in *Being and Nothingness*." In *Jean-Paul Sartre: Contemporary Approaches to His Philosophy*, edited by Hugh J. Silverman and Frederick A. Elliston, 50–62. Brighton, Sussex: Harvester Press, 1980.

Morris, Phyllis Sutton. "Sartre on the Self-Deceiver's Translucent Consciousness." *Journal of the British Society for Phenomenology* 23, no. 2 (May 1992): 103–19.

Murphy, Julien S. "The Look in Sartre and Rich." In *The Thinking Muse: Feminism and Modern French Philosophy*, edited by Jeffner Allen and Iris Marion Young, 101–12. Bloomington: Indiana University Press, 1989.

Neu, Jerome. "Divided Minds: Sartre's 'Bad Faith' Critique of Freud." *Review of Metaphysics* 42, no. 1 (September 1988): 79–101.

Nixon, Sean. "Exhibiting Masculinity." In *Representation: Cultural Representation and Signifying Practices*, edited by Stuart Hall, 291–330. London: Sage, 1997.

Salvan, Jaques. *To Be and Not To Be: An Analysis of Jean-Paul Sartre's Ontology*. Detroit: Wayne State University Press, 1962.

Santoni, Ronald E. *Bad Faith, Good Faith and Authenticity in Sartre's Early Philosophy*. Philadelphia: Temple University Press, 1995.

Sartre, Jean-Paul. *Anti-Semite and Jew*. Translated by George. J. Becker. New York: Schocken Books, 1948.

———. *Being and Nothingness: An Essay on Phenomenological Ontology*. Translated by Hazel E. Barnes. London: Routledge, 1958.

———. "The Childhood of a Leader." In *Intimacy*, translated by Lloyd Alexander, 130–220. London: Panther Books, 1960.

———. "Consciousness of Self and Knowledge of Self." In *Readings in Existential Phenomenology*, edited by Nathaniel Lawrence and Daniel O'Connor, 113–42. Englewood Cliffs, N.J.: Prentice-Hall, 1967.

———. *Critique of Dialectical Reason*. Volume 1. Translated by Alan Sheridan-Smith. London: Verso, 1991.

———. *The Emotions: Outline of a Theory*. Translated by Bernard Frechtman. Secaucus, N.J.: Citadel Press, 1975.

———. *Existentialism and Humanism*. Translated by Philip Mairet. London: Methuen, 1948.

———. "Intentionality: A Fundamental Idea of Husserl's Phenomenology." Translated by Joseph. P. Fell. *The Journal of the British Society for Phenomenology* 1, no. 2 (May 1970): 4–5.

———. *Notebooks for an Ethics*. Translated by David Pellauer. Chicago: University of Chicago Press, 1992.

———. *The Transcendence of the Ego: An Existentialist Theory of Consciousness*. Translated by Forrest Williams and Robert Kirkpatrick. New York: Noonday Press, 1957.

Solomon, Robert. "Sartre on Emotions." In *The Philosophy of Jean-Paul Sartre*, edited by Paul Arthur Schilpp, 211–28. La Salle, Ill.: Open Court, 1981.

Warnock, Mary. *The Philosophy of Sartre*. London: Hutchinson, 1965.

Weberman, David. "Sartre, Emotions, and Wallowing." *American Philosophical Quarterly* 33, no. 4 (October 1996): 393–407.

Wilson, R. McL. "Mani and Manichaeism." In *The Encyclopedia of Philosophy*, volume 5, edited by Paul Edwards, 149–50. New York: Macmillan and Free Press, 1967.

Wolf, Naomi. *The Beauty Myth*. London: Vintage, 1990.

Wood, Allen W. "Self-Deception and Bad Faith." In *Perspectives on Self-Deception*, edited by Brian P. McLaughlin and Amélie Oksenberg Rorty, 207–27. Berkeley and Los Angeles: University of California Press, 1988.

Young, Iris Marion. *Justice and the Politics of Difference*. Princeton, N.J.: Princeton University Press, 1990.

Index

absence, 5. *See also* dichotomy: bodily absence/bodily presence
ambiguity of the human condition, xii, 1, 6, 22, 25, 34, 41, 43–44, 48, 93, 100–101, 105 119n5, 121, 125, 133, 136. *See also* bad faith: and the human condition
analytic spirit, 61, 63, 79
Anderson, Thomas, 23, 27n33, 27n39, 119n4, 119n11
anger, 65, 71, 73–74, 76–77
anguish, 15–17, 41, 98
anti-Semite. *See* anti-Semitism
Anti-Semite and Jew (Sartre), xiii, 59–60, 71–72, 80–81, 87, 89n4, 90n8, 111, 113–15, 120n18
anti-Semitism, xii–xiv, 59, 77– 89, 89n1, 93–94, 106, 120n22, 139, 141; and belief, 61, 64; collective, 111–18; and equality, 113–14; individual, 60, 111–12, 118; justifications for, 62; the role of opinion in, 60–63, 79, 89n2; and passion, 61–62, 64, 71–72, 78, 82,

84, 86, 88; predisposition toward, 62. *See also* bad faith: and anti-Semitism; Manichaeism; us-object: anti-Semite and the
Appiah, Kwame Anthony, 92n39
Aryan, 64, 82, 114–116
authenticity, 29–30, 39, 87, 104–5, 112, 119n12

bad faith: and anti-Semitism, 63, 78–80, 83–84, 86, 89, 92n37, 93, 117–18; beliefs, 43–44, 47–48, 51, 54–55, 64, 84–85, 104; and collectivity, xii, 106, 110, 112–13; defined, xii, 29; denial of facticity, xii-xiv, 39–43, 48, 59, 78, 103, 106, 118, 126, 136, 138, 140–41; and the human condition, xii, 24, 30–43, 78, 93, 100, 122, 126, 133, 136; instability of, 54, 135; and intersubjectivity, xii, xiv, 94, 101–5; and oppression, xi-xiv, 29, 59, 93, 139–41, 141n2; and the past,

149

About the Author

Thomas Martin was raised and educated in Australia. He first became interested in the work of Sartre when he was a graduate student at Flinders University of South Australia, and went on to complete a doctoral dissertation on Sartrean philosophy at the University of New South Wales. He has continued his research on Sartre in his current position as lecturer in the Department of Philosophy, Rhodes University, South Africa.

Learning Resources
Centre